After Tomorrow the Days Disappear

NORTHWESTERN WORLD CLASSICS

*Northwestern World Classics brings readers
the world's greatest literature. The series features
essential new editions of well-known works,
lesser-known books that merit reconsideration,
and lost classics of fiction, drama, and poetry.
Insightful commentary and compelling new translations
help readers discover the joy of outstanding writing
from all regions of the world.*

Hasan Sijzi of Delhi

After Tomorrow
the Days Disappear
Ghazals and Other Poems

Translated from the Persian
by Rebecca Gould

Northwestern University Press ✦ *Evanston, Illinois*

Northwestern University Press
www.nupress.northwestern.edu

Printed in the United States of America

10 9 8 7 6 5 4 3 2 1

Library of Congress Cataloging-in-Publication Data

Hasan Dihlavi, 1253 or 1254–approximately 1338, author.
    [Poems. Selections. English]
    After tomorrow the days disappear : ghazals and other poems / Hasan
Sijzi of Delhi ; translated from the Persian by Rebecca Gould.
        pages cm — (Northwestern World Classics)
    Includes bibliographical references.
    ISBN 978-0-8101-3230-6 (pbk. : alk. paper) —
ISBN 978-0-8101-3231-3 (ebook)
    I. Gould, Rebecca Ruth, translator. II. Title. III. Series: Northwestern
world classics.
    PK6470.H338A2 2016
    891'.5511—dc23

                                                            2015034910

for Beth Anna Gould, dreamer, sister, friend

*What pleases in a ghazal is the variety with which
conspicuous sameness can be sustained; what the
form unleashes is the poet's mercurial powers.*
—Kelly LeFave, American poet

One of the most distinctive and recognizable features of Persian po-
etics, the refrain (*radīf*), entered literary history by way of a contrast
with Arabic poetic norms. Defined as a word, syllable, or set of syl-
lables that recurs at the conclusion of each poetic distich (couplet),
radīf can be provisionally translated as "refrain." As a slightly more
technical definition has it, the *radīf* is "a word or words supplement-
ing and following the rhyme proper and occurring without change
at the end of each line."[1] Notwithstanding these descriptions, the
radīf does more than simply recur, and its very repetitions generate
change.[2] Toward the end of the twelfth century, the Persian poet-
critic Rashīd al-Dīn Vaṭvāṭ dedicated a special section of his rhetori-
cal treatise, *Gardens of Magic in the Nuances of Poetry*, to explaining
this literary device. Defining the *radīf* as one or more words that
recur after the rhyme, Vaṭvāṭ noted that Arabic poets "do not use
radīfs, except for recent innovators displaying their virtuosity."[3] El-
evating the Persian refrain to the gold standard of poetic excellence,
Vaṭvāṭ argued that this device effectively tests the poet's talent (*ṭab'*)
and excellence (*basṭat*).

Even as the formalization of the *radīf* within the Persian literary-
critical tradition was heralded by rhetoricians, Persian poets turned
increasingly to this literary device to develop the resources of the
Persian literary language as it defined itself against—and within—
Arabic poetic genres. In nontechnical terms, the *radīf* functions
like a song's refrain, with the difference that the rules governing its
usage are more formalized than in many musical and performance
traditions. When it occurs, the poetic *radīf* is found at the end of
every distich, and twice in the first distich. The *radīf* can be seen as

an extended version of the rhyme letter (known in Persian as the *ravī* or the *ḥarf-i qāfīye*) that concludes every line of Persian verse, including those translated in this volume, yet it is also another kind of entity, one that carries semantic value.[4] Although, like any rhyme, it intensifies the sonic resonance of a verse, the *radīf* is often more complex, more semantically weighted, and more formally demanding than the rhymes that inform Anglophone poetics. Not all Persian poems have *radīfs*, but those that do are distinctive, each in its own way.

As a Persian contribution to comparative poetics, the *radīf* constitutes one of this tradition's major contributions to world literature. But what does the *radīf* do for us today? How can it help us savor the nuances of literary form, and make sense of the wide travels of the Persian *ghazal* across languages, cultures, and continents? Before exploring these questions, we would do well to dwell on the life and times of the writer who cultivated the *radīf* in Persianate South Asia with greater sophistication than any of his predecessors. The writer in question is Hasan Sijzi, whose poems are translated in this volume, which marks his first book-length appearance in English.

Hasan Sijzi's World

Hasan Sijzi entered the world at a moment when Persian culture in India had yet to become Indo-Persian in the sense that this term is understood today. More global than local, his literary culture was in many respects indistinguishable from Persian culture elsewhere in the eastern Islamic world. Although the literary form called the *ghazal* already had a long history in Arabic and Persian literature, it had yet to make a major impact on the Indian subcontinent.[5] Mongol invasions (alluded to in *rubāʿī* 15) had hastened the collapse of Baghdad's waning caliphate in 1258, and created vacuums of power for the new Perso-Turkic dynasties that were appearing across South and Central Asia. The panegyric ode (*qaṣīda*) had to compete for eminence in the Persian genre system with newly emergent lyric genres, including the *ghazal* and the *rubāʿī* (quatrain). (This collection includes examples of each genre, with an emphasis on lyric forms.)

In Hasan's world, the composition of poetry was entangled in contestations of political sovereignty, even as the poetry of patronage was giving way to the verse of mystic union. The literary idiom cultivated by Hasan and his contemporaries viewed spiritual longing through the prism of worldly desire, as can be seen by the many meanings attached to erotic desire in the poems translated here.[6] These developments within Persian literature, in particular the shift from the court to the Sufi lodge (*khanqah*) and the school of flattery to the discourse of the heart, cannot be separated from historical shifts in literary production and the new sources of political power. Like other poets of the Delhi Sultanate (1206–1526), Hasan left a *dīvān* (collected verse) rich in panegyric odes, but it is his lyric verse that has earned him permanent renown.

Like many other poets, critics, and historians who attained prominence in the Delhi Sultanate, Hasan descended from immigrants who had journeyed to South Asia while fleeing the Mongol invasions and had taken up residence in Delhi in search of new opportunities and a peaceful existence. While there are conflicting accounts regarding the location of his birth, it is known that Hasan passed most of his adult life in Delhi.[7] During the years that Hasan entered poetic maturity, the city of Delhi was "renowned throughout the Islamic world for its institutions of learning and as a haven for wandering scholars and poets."[8]

The poet's full name, Amīr Najm al-Dīn Ḥasan Dihlavī ibn Khwāja ʿAlā al-Dīn Sistānī, indicates that his father was from Sistān (also known as Sijistān), an area that encompassed eastern Iran and southern Afghanistan. Hence his name Sijzi, meaning from Sijistān.[9] According to his own testimony, Hasan began writing poetry at the age of thirteen. His major influences included the Persian poets Saʿdī (d. 1291), best known as the author of *Gulistān* (Rose Garden) but also a pioneer of the *ghazal* form, and the mystically inclined author of many quatrains (*rubāʿiyyat*) Abū Saʿīd Abū al-Khayr (d. 1049).[10] While still a youth, Hasan became publicly known for his verse. His trajectory to fame began with his encounter with Delhi's most famous poet, Amīr Khusrow, at a baker's shop in the city. When the sixteenth-century historian Firishta described the meeting of the two poets, he referred to Hasan as Khwāja (teacher), a title by which he was known for much of subsequent history. As the title suggests, by the early modern period Hasan was regarded as central both to Indo-Persian literature and to the history of Indian Sufism. Firishta's account continues, as he explores the dynamic between the two poets, as well as their mutual relation to the man who was to be their most important teacher, Shaykh Niẓām al-Dīn (1238–1325):

> One day Shaykh Niẓām al-Dīn Awliyā' was passing through the marketplace with his companions, among whom was Amīr Khusrow, then in the prime of his youth. Khwāja Hasan, the poet, who was extremely handsome and a perfect master of excellence, was sitting at the counter of a baker's shop. When Amīr Khusrow saw him, he found him to be elegant, with a graceful and attractive nature. Captivated by his image, he went to the shop and asked, "How do you sell your bread?" Hasan replied, "I put the bread on one scale of the balance and ask the customer to put his money on the other, when the money overweighs, I allow the customer to go." Amīr Khusrow said, "If the customer has no money what would you do?" Hasan replied, "I accept his regret and supplication in place of gold." Amīr Khusrow was astonished by this reply and reported it to Shaykh Niẓām al-Dīn. Hasan was also captivated by the Shaykh, and left his job that same day. Even before Hasan became a disciple of the Shaykh, he frequented his lodge and dedicated himself to the acquisition of knowledge. From this time, as the story goes, there developed a great friendship between the two poets.[11]

In addition to what it tells us about the friendship between these two most important poets of the Delhi Sultanate, this anecdote is important as a record of Hasan's introduction to Shaykh Niẓām al-Dīn, whose sayings he was eventually to collect into a volume.[12] *Rubāʿī* 17 of this volume, which addresses a person named "Khusrow," suggests that the deep friendship between the two poets was affected by rivalry during certain periods of its duration. This anecdote reveals the affection and indeed attraction that also marked their acquaintance. Finally, the anecdote is important as a statement of the values that underwrote the triangular relationship among the Sufi master and his two disciples, Hasan and Amīr Khusrow: each was implicitly linked to the others through a vow of poverty that, while it did not exclude courtly patronage, kept its distance from the pomp and majesty of courtly life.[13] Although Firishta recorded this encounter at a remove of several centuries, he drew on deep historical memories. In preserving this story of the first meeting between the two great Persian poets of fourteenth-century Hindustan (Hasan and Amīr Khusrow), Firishta announces a beginning of sorts for Indo-Persian literature—that is, a Persian literary tradition and a cultural identity that defines itself with reference to South Asia.

Over the course of many decades of collaboration and, as *rubāʿī* 17 suggests, incipient rivalry, Hasan and Amīr Khusrow ascended to fame in the politically fraught environment of Sultanate Delhi. Amīr Khusrow died in 1325, the same year as their teacher and spiritual guide, Niẓām al-Dīn, and was buried next to him in the Niẓām al-Dīn *dargāh* (mausoleum) in Delhi. By contrast with the well-known story of Amīr Khusrow's demise following the death of Niẓām al-Dīn, the circumstances of Hasan's death have yet to be ascertained. Two Mughal-era historians, Badāʾūnī and Firishta, state that Hasan died in Dawlatabad (Deogir) in South India, after Sultan Muhammad Tughluq relocated there in 1327 as a precautionary measure following the Mongol invasions.[14] Hasan's death in Dawlatabad, which had become the Sultanate's second capital, probably occurred within a decade of his relocation, and dates have been given ranging from 1328 to 1336.

ʿAbd al-Raḥmān Chishtī (d. 1683), a member of the same Sufi order to which Hasan belonged, corroborates the historians' accounts. He states that Hasan was buried "at Deogir, near the sepulcher of shaykh Burhan al-Din Gharib," another disciple of Niẓām al-Dīn.[15] "His tomb," the text continues, "is a place of pilgrimage to the people of that country who call him Ḥasan Shīr [Hasan the Lion] because no one can stay near his tomb at night." Anyone who attempted to stay overnight would be overcome by "a vision of a lion" and would "fall into a swoon." As this local memory attests, Hasan's legacy persisted for centuries after his death, particularly within Sufi circles and among devotees of Persian poetry. As a poet, Hasan set his sights higher than did the typical courtier. He used his poetic gifts to illuminate the metaphysics of nothingness, to bring mystical experience into contact with worldly yearning, and to give verbal form to mortal existence. Alongside his literary legacy, he became a sacred figure in Chishtī historiography.

Together, Amīr Khusrow and Hasan Sijzi extended the boundaries of Persian literature, in part by incorporating Indic content into their verse. Their merger of Persianate and Indian narrative traditions—and even, in the case of Amīr Khusrow, the use of poetic devices and words from Indian vernaculars—marked a turning point in Persian literary history.[16] That Hasan remained more fully within a strictly Persian aesthetic may account in part for the neglect of his poetry in later centuries, when readers were more interested in vernacular (Hindustani, Awadhi) than in Persian literature. Recognized or not, the techniques and aesthetic of Hasan and Amīr Khusrow set the stage for the multilingual and cross-confessional innovation of later centuries. Perhaps most notably, Hasan's narrative poem 'Ishqnāma (*Book of Desire*) is one of the earliest self-proclaimed adaptations of an Indian story to a Persian narrative form.[17]

Sameness in Difference, Difference in Sameness

Among the *ghazals* included in this collection that use the *radīf* in innovative ways, Ghazal 1, with the *radīf judā*, strikingly exemplifies the literary possibilities of this device:

دو روز شد که شدم زان مه یگانه جدا
همه نشاط شد از تن بدین بهانه جدا
منم بناله زار از در جدای دوست
چو زار ناله و مرغی ز آشیانه جدا
ز تیر غمزه او کشته گشت بین شهری
که هست سر پیکانش را نشانه جدا

زمانه قصد بخون می کند ستاره به جان

غم جدایی آن دلبریگانه جدا

چه طالع ست مرا کین چنین کشندم زار

غمش جدا و ستاره جدا زمانه جدا

یکی رعایت حال حسن کنید که ماند

ز یار دور ز دل بی خبر ز خانه جدا

(*Dīvān-i Amīr Ḥasan Sijzī Dihlavī*, 128)

Since my lover parted two days have passed.
Every joy left this body when he parted.
Like a bird torn from its nest, I lament
separation from my beloved's door.
When life was severed from the body,
it became impossible to part from the beloved's door.
Observe the city, killed by the arrow of my lover's glance:
Signs of parting puncture the arrow's tips.
Time yearns for blood, while the grief
of my beloved's departure is killed by stars.
Since it is my fate to be killed by grief,
I am severed from sorrow, stars, and time.
Observe Hasan: far from his beloved,
unaware of his heart, far from home.

In Persian, the *ghazal* depends for its effect on the repetition of the *radīf judā*, the semantic spectrum of which includes "parted," "separate," "distinct," and "divided," at the end of every couplet. My rendering of this *radīf* seeks to reproduce its effect in translation by offering several variations on *judā*, a word that bears considerable semantic flexibility in Persian. Thus, when the lover "parted," the poet is spurred by his "departure," even though only one Persian term is used for these different meanings. (In some cases, meanings proliferate in the opposite direction; consider the many words in Hasan's vocabulary for "hair," a diversity that an English translation must inconveniently condense into a few terms: "locks," "curls," "hair.") Arrows pierce the poet with yet more "signs of parting," and the lover's "separation" is compared to time's "departure," even though the Persian *radīf* remains constant. The variations on "parting" used in this *ghazal* correspond to a single word (*judā*); while the English rendering necessarily introduces a degree of variation, it does preserve the refrain's repetitive effect.

The full power of the *radīf judā* is activated in the concluding verse (technically known as the *maqṭaʿ*), with the introduction of the second defining feature of the Persian *ghazal* and another key element in the contribution of Persian literature to global poetics, the pen name (*takhalluṣ*).[18] In keeping with the *ghazal* form as it had been standardized by the thirteenth century, the poet refers to himself in the third person, while at the same time addressing an imagined listener/reader, whom he calls on to cast his gaze (*rāʿyat*) on Hasan and to observe the poet's destitute condition: far from his lover (*yār dūr*), bewildered (*bī khabar*), and severed from his home (*ze khāneh judā*). In this instance, the authorial positioning afforded by the *takhalluṣ* is internal to the signification of the refrain, for the alienation of self and other that is implicit in such forms of authorial reference is literally entailed in the meaning of *judā*. In this way, the Persian refrain enables content to express form and form to express content.

Beyond this specific example, another significant function of the *takhalluṣ* within Persian poetics was its conferral of fame on the poet. A poet's *takhalluṣ* provided the formal testimony of his position "at the court of the patrons for whose soirées his songs were composed."[19] This observation, made with respect to the Ghaznavid poet Sanāʾī (d. 1131), also clarifies the creative power wielded by the *takhalluṣ* at the court in Delhi. In particular, it sheds light on one of Hasan's most paradoxical *ghazals*, number 14 in this collection, on the *radīf ke mīgūyad ke nīst* (that is said to not exist). This poem ends by deploying the *takhalluṣ* in a quite striking way. The *maqṭaʿ* (concluding verse) invokes the title of the ruler ʿAlā al-Dīn Khiljī (r. 1296–1316), referred to as *shāh*, in place of the name of the poet, which would normally occur in the concluding verse:

A shah served by one hundred servants
is like a *khaqan* and known as God. This is true.
The servant in front of you
is like a hundred *khaqan*s. This is untrue.

Alongside the replacement of the poet's name by the title of his ruler is a possible allusion to the poet Khāqānī (d. 1199), famed for his elaborate poetics, with the invocation of *khaqan*. Even as the poet's name is made interchangeable with that of his patron, this proximity to another poet's *takhalluṣ* suggests another kind of controvertibility. Rather than signifying poetic genius, as Khāqānī often did in Indo-Persian literary texts, this invocation points to a sycophant.[20] The elision of a conventional *takhalluṣ* achieves an effect here even more powerful than its inclusion could have done in figuring Hasan as unique among his peers for his relative distance from the patronage network. At the same time, this *ghazal* on the *radīf* "that is said to not exist" never surrenders its panegyric ambitions, for its raison d'être is the praise of Shah 'Alā al-Dīn. These complex significations, each of which is dependent on the presence or absence of the *takhalluṣ*, demonstrate that, for the purposes of poetic meaning, what is omitted can matter more than what is said.

With only a few exceptions, each of the fifty *ghazals* included here give the poet's *takhalluṣ* in the concluding verse (only *ghazals* 2 and 17 give it slightly earlier). The *ghazals* that omit the *takhalluṣ* do so for a reason. In the example given above, the substitution of the poet's name with that of the shah has political salience. In another exception, *ghazal* 49, the elision of the poet's name serves the poem's purpose of rhetorically denigrating the poet's persona and encouraging his lover to leave. While the verses between the opening verse (*maṭla'*) and the concluding verse (*maqta'*) may be loosely structured, and there are few regulations in terms of their content, the opening and closing verses of the *ghazal* stringently submit to a fixed pattern: the *radīf* must occur twice in the *maṭla'*, halfway through and at the close of each distich, and the *takhalluṣ* must occur in the *maqta'*, generally toward the beginning. To the extent that I have rendered Hasan's *takhalluṣ* in his concluding verses and his *radīfs* in his opening verses, I have preserved this pattern in my translations. When I have diverged from the original—occasionally by placing the *radīf* at the beginning of each verse rather than at the end, where Persian poetic norms require it to be—the intent has been to convey the effect of the Persian device through means that resonate more sonorously in English.

In the history of the *ghazal*, the unvarying *radīf* has often been rendered in translation through patterned variation. For example, the German orientalist Hammer-Purgstall rendered one of Hafez's *ghazals* on the *radīf āmad* (comes) by alternating between *gekommen* (to come) and *bekommen* (to get).[21] By adhering, like Hammer-Purgstall, to the principle of sameness in difference and difference in sameness, I have endeavored to convey the poetic force of the original without retrofitting the Persian text into an English structure that makes an overuse of rhyme sound monotonous.

Other of Hasan's *ghazals* do more with the refrain than simply letting it close each distich. In addition to reproducing the *radīf* at the end of each distich, these poems incorporate it elsewhere in the text. One example is *ghazal* 40, which makes ingenious use of the letter *nūn*. *Nūn* is a letter of the Persian alphabet (ن), as well as the final syllable for many Persian words. Here, it is a rhyming letter (Arabic *ravī*; Persian *ḥarf-i qāfīye*) that serves a function parallel to the *radīf*, without quite constituting a *radīf* as such in that it is not a complete word or phrase. (While I have listed the *radīf* for every *ghazal* that has one in my translations, with *ghazal* 40, as elsewhere that such non-*radīf* rhyming occurs, I have left the recurring letter or sound unmarked.)

بی لعل لبت پرشد چشمم ز در مکنون
ای مردمک دیده آخر نظری اکنون
ابروی تو خوش نقشی و آن خال برآن بالا
نون شد مگر ابرویت و آن خال نقطه برنون
قانون طبیبان است عم خوردن بیماران
من ز جان بدهم پیشت گر نگزری از قانون
لیلی صفت از ناقه رانی بسوی کعبه
اصحاب حرم بینی دیوانه تر از ماجنون
هردم چو حسن آرم از دیده و دل پیشت
اشکی چو عقیق تر نظمی چو در مکنون

(*Dīvān-i Amīr Ḥasan Sijzī Dihlavī*, 489)

Lacking the ruby of your lips, my eyes filled with secret pearls.
Pupil of the eye, cast your glance again.
Your brow is etched well, as carefully as the mole above.

Your brows form the letter *nūn* (ن), and the mole above is its dot.
The doctors legislate that the sick ones suffer from pain.
I will surrender my soul in front of you if you reject this law.
Oh, Laylī, you drive your followers' camels toward the Ka'ba.
You see how the guardians of the shrine are crazier than Majnūn.
All the while, Hasan, I bring my eyes and heart in front of you.
My tears are redder than agate. My heart's disposition is a hidden
    door.

Ghazal 40 uses words ending in *n* (the Persian *nūn*) throughout. For
example, *qānūn* (law) occurs twice in the second distich and at the
beginning of the third. Using *nūn* as the rhyming letter enables the
poet to include other rhyming words, such as *aknūn* ("now," v. 1),
maknūn ("hidden, latent," v. 1 and 5), and, most compellingly, *maj-
nūn* (v. 4). While this last word can be translated simply as "mad-
ness," Majnūn is also the famed lover of Laylī. According to the
Arabic legend that entered Persian through oral sources, Majnūn
loved Laylī more than any other lover has ever loved his beloved.
Majnūn's devotion to his beloved features regularly in classical Per-
sian poetry.[22] When the poet claims in the fourth distich that the
guardians (*āṣḥāb*) of the shrine (*ḥaram*) are crazier than Majnūn, he
is therefore claiming that such attraction can overturn the social or-
der, so that even the pious find themselves beholden to worldly de-
sire. Meanwhile, the poet remains calm in the face of such chaos, for
his immersion in poetry enables him to focus on the hidden door,
which signifies an opening into eternity.

The power of these verses is compounded by a double entendre
(*īhām*) that attends *ḥaram* (shrine). Vocalized differently, *ḥaram*
can also be read as *ḥarim*, meaning the place where women lived
in premodern Islamic societies (the spelling is the same). Since the
Ka'ba was a shrine, the signification of *ḥarim* is only latent. Still, this
secondary meaning adds another layer to this poetic image. Hasan's
use of the rhyming letter *nūn* in this *ghazal* extends poetic meaning
by bringing incongruous significations into rhyming relations. To
adapt W. H. Auden, the end result of such technical feats is a "sound
metaphor," a verbal congruence that acquires semantic meaning
through phonemic proximity.[23]

The Poetics of Incongruity

Due to a paucity of naturally sonorous end-rhymes in English, the translator who aims to preserve the *radīf* in translation is compelled to yoke seemingly incongruous objects together. In part, this tendency was already latent within Persian poetics, particularly among poets who participated in the school of elaborate poetics that later came to be called the Indian style (*sabk-i hindī*). Alessandro Bausani alludes to this shift in poetic values when he speaks of how "the shattering of the law of formal harmony" becomes more marked, the closer the *ghazal* approaches to modernity.[24]

I have noted that *ghazals* with the most commonplace refrains tend to be most resistant to translation. This principle holds for the five *rubāʿīs* included in this volume; only when there is a semantic rhyme in the original—a *radīf* in the strict sense of the term—has this repetition been reproduced in translation. As this pattern shows, while it may be the case that, to invoke Robert Frost, poetry is what gets lost in translation, the *radīf* adheres to another law, of the translatability of all things human. In the felicitous moments of working on these translations, phonemic and conceptual fidelity occurred together thanks to the semantic quality of the *radīf* and its compound nature. Simple or conventional *radīfs*, and rhyming letters with non-semantic content, offer less that can make the journey from one language to another. Firmly rooted in a specific idiom, these words and phrases are more closely yoked to the languages from which they emerge than their more amorphous and malleable counterparts.

Before undertaking this translation of Hasan's *ghazals*, I expected that the *radīfs* that demanded the least from the Persian poet would lend themselves most readily to English translation. In keeping with the logic of Frost's dictum, such *radīfs* would seem to have less to lose over the course of their linguistic metamorphoses. The opposite turned out to be the case: the *radīfs* that had the most to lose in translation also benefited the most from being transported into new linguistic worlds.

Among the *radīfs* in the *ghazals* translated here that most fully demonstrate the gains made by translation are *farāmūsh* (forgotten), *al-widā'* ("farewell" in Arabic), *'ishq* (desire, love), *gūyīm* (we/I say), *raftam* (I went), *dīl* (heart), *nevīsam* (I write), *nimīpursīm* (we/I don't ask), *nadāram* (I don't have), *nadārad* (does not have), *nimīravad* (will not pass), *dīrīnih* (ancient), *chegūneh* (what kind), *mībīnam* (I see), *bud man dānestam* (I knew), and *nimīdānistam* (I didn't know).[25] My endeavors to render these extended *radīfs* into English confirmed a counterintuitive hypothesis advanced by Walter Benjamin.[26] The closer a text approaches to mere information (*Mitteilung*)—meaning, in this context, the simpler the refrain's grammatical function—the more, to Benjamin's mind, it will resist translation, because simpler *radīfs* are less prone to generate polysemy.[27] Benjamin's point is that texts that foreground language's polysemy are translatable (*übersetzbar*), compared to texts that conceal or suppress polysemy for the sake of communicating information. Translatability thus becomes a benchmark of a reflexivity that is literary as well as conceptual, rather than a measure of clarity or transparency in language. Over the course of my work on the *ghazal*, the *radīf* became for me a measure of a *ghazal*'s translatability, and I came to expect that the most complex and daring of Hasan's *radīfs* would lend themselves most fully to the journey across languages.

The translatability of the *radīf* bears equally on the work it does within Persian poetics and on its life in translation. If the Persian refrain's propensity to link incongruous objects is translatable in ways that elude non-semantic rhyme, then the relevance of the Persian lyric to the study of literary form becomes clear. The translatability of the *radīf* supports Benjamin's assertion that the "fixed meaning [*bestimmte Bedeutung*] residing in the original text expresses itself" through the act of translation.[28] The *radīf* perfectly exemplifies fixed meaning in this sense, for its structure and content cannot change. Conceptualizing translation as the art of transferring a fixed, rather than an indeterminate, meaning from one language into another causes us to think differently about the relationship between meaning and form, as well as to think anew about the value of constraints in the creative process. In Benjamin's account, form is what is translated, rather than meaning, which has no fixed form. While form inheres (*innewohnt*) within the original text, because it also conditions its very existence, the text does not contain or constrain the form. Translation makes visible the fixity of form, and reveals how it crosses the semantic and phonemic divide between languages. The translatable *radīf* is a kind of metaphor—a "carrying over," as the Greek meaning of *metaphora* suggests—between two (and sometimes more than two) linguistic worlds. While its form makes it translatable, its semantic quality makes it worth translating in the first place.

As a formal device bearing a peculiar relationship to translation, the translatability of the *radīf* is key to the *ghazal*'s "wide and deep influence on the literatures of Asia," which has been the subject of multiple studies.[29] The influence of the Persian *ghazal* persists into our Anglophone present, with the verse of Agha Shahid Ali, Adrienne Rich, Mimi Khalvati, W. S. Merwin, Maxine Kumin, and John Hollander, each of whom have pioneered the English *ghazal* in different ways. This influence encompasses the literatures of Albania, the Malay Archipelago, and the Deccan, to list merely a few of the many geographies the *ghazal* genre has traversed, thanks in part to Hasan's labors and imagination. Within Iran itself, Hasan's influence on pioneers of the later Persian *ghazal*, including Ḥāfeẓ, Khvāju Kirmānī, and Zamīrī of Isfahan, attests to the centrality of his oeuvre, and of his chosen genre, to Persian and world literature. (Indeed Zamīrī produced a book-length imitation of Hasan's poetry at the Safavid court.) The contemporary Tajik scholar Lola Salomatshaeva argues that Hasan's poetics generated an entire school of lyricists in Persian from the fourteenth to the seventeenth centuries, a group that included Kamāl Khujandī, Zayn al-Dīn al-Vāṣifī, Faizī, and 'Abd al-Raḥmān Mushfiqī.[30] In light of these influences, Hasan's legacy supports one scholar's assertion that "it is in the art of the ghazal . . . that Indo-Persian poets produced their most subtle innovations."[31]

Situated between the language of the original and another language's shore, the Persian refrain is an object lesson for translation studies generally. If translation is, in Benjamin's words, a "provisional way of coming to terms with the foreignness of languages," the *radīf* is the ideal instrument for making the difference-in-sameness, among ourselves and within our languages, visible and available to others for reflection.[32] In giving flesh to sounds, Hasan's *radīfs* remind us of the incongruity of all comparisons. In forcing us to face the incommensurability between language and its object, this poet compels us to confront the breach between self and other, and being and non-being—the keynote of Persian poetics, particularly in a poetics as influenced by Sufi teachings as was Hasan's. Although Hasan is original within the Persian literary tradition for other reasons as well, the *radīf* is the key formal device that made his literary innovations possible.

The reader who compares these verses to the Persian originals (a task that will be aided by the tables at the end, which list where the poems occur in the two recent editions) will have occasion to observe certain peculiarities of my translational method. When it seemed impossible to render specific verses satisfactorily into English, I have cut them from the translation. This practice seemed justified in light of the manuscript culture within which Hasan worked, in which the sequence of specific verses varied from manuscript to manuscript, and verses were added and omitted according to the scribe's inclinations. As for many manuscript cultures, the notion of a definitive urtext not susceptible to change, from which all later scribal accretions can be washed away, is a conceptual impossibility for Persian literature, notwithstanding the central role played by this ideal within the European philological tradition.[33]

Even as I have omitted certain verses for convenience's sake, I have anchored these translations in the original Persian by providing the *radīf* in Persian and roman script and in English translation. With the *radīf* at hand, the Anglophone reader will have better access to the driving force of the original.[34] Another benefit of including the *radīf* is that it enables the non-Persianist to compare the English versions with the structure of the original, since the reader will be able to see when and where the *radīf* is reproduced even without accessing it in Persian. Where no *radīf* is listed, this means that the poem in question only makes use of a non-semantic rhyming letter.

The 50 *ghazals* that follow are but a sample, albeit the most extensive to date in English, of the 901 *ghazals* included in the Tehran edition.[35] I have added seventeen quatrains (*rubāʿiyyat*), two fragments (*qiṭaʿāt*), and one ode (*qaṣīda*) to this selection of Hasan's *ghazals* to give the reader a sense of his poetic range. I have left the other poetic genres to which Hasan contributed, most notably the verse narrative (*masnavī*), for another occasion.

Each of the seventy poems presented is an interpretation in the sense of poet-translator Geoffrey Squires, who used this term to describe his recent and widely acclaimed translations of Hafez.[36] Like the *ghazal* itself, no translation is ever complete. When the poet asks himself in the concluding verse to *ghazal* 16: "Hasan, why are you not mindful here? / After tomorrow the days disappear," he enfolds the mutability of time into his poetic self. The contingency of mortal life profoundly influenced Hasan's way of conceiving the composition of poetry, as well as of understanding its place in the world. Equally the result of his Sufi convictions, his love of language, and his desire for life itself, Hasan's poems showcase the *ghazal*'s unique contribution to world literature.

Notes

The epigraph is taken from LeFave's unpublished letter, dated October 10, 1999, to Agha Shahid Ali, cited in the latter's introduction to *Ravishing DisUnities: Real Ghazals in English* (Hanover, N.H.: Wesleyan University Press, 2000), 3.

1. Laurence Paul Elwell-Sutton, *The Persian Metres* (Cambridge: Cambridge University Press, 1976), 225.

2. I use *distich* and *couplet* interchangeably here to refer to the *bayt*, which is the basic unit of Persian and Arabic verse, equivalent to the English distich in that it is divided into two parts, each of which are called *miṣrā's*. While the *bayt* is unfixed with respect to meter or syllable length, the key requirement is that both of its components are identical in structure.

3. Rashīd al-Dīn Vaṭvāṭ, *Ḥadā'iq al-siḥr fī daqā'iq al-shi'r*, ed. 'Abbās Iqbāl (Tehran: Sanā'ī, 1404/1984), 315.

4. For the earlier phases of the Arabic and Persian *ghazal*, see the works of Jacobi, Kinany, and Fatima in the bibliography at the end of this volume.

5. For this range of meanings in the *ghazal*, see Domenico Ingenito, "Tabrizis in Shiraz Are Worth Less than a Dog: Sa'dī and Humām, a Lyrical Encounter," in *Politics, Patronage and the Transmission of Knowledge*

in *13th–15th Century Tabriz*, ed. Judith Pfeiffer (Leiden: Brill, 2014), especially 102.

6. Although M. I. Borah ("The Life and Works of Amir Hasan Dihlavi," *Journal of the Royal Asiatic Society of Bengal* 7 [1941]: 1) asserts that Hasan was born in Delhi, Lola Salomatshaeva cites a verse, missing from other Persian editions, in which the poet states that he was born in Badaun, 200 kilometers southeast of Delhi. See the introduction to her edition of Hasan's *Divan* (Dushanbe: Irfon, 1990), 6.

7. Sunil Sharma and Paul Losensky, "Introduction," in *In the Bazaar of Love: The Selected Poetry of Amir Khusrau* (Delhi: Penguin Books India, 2011), xxiv.

8. Borah argues that the other name by which the poet was known, Sanjarī, was a scribal error for Sistānī ("The Life and Works," 1n1).

9. Borah, "The Life and Works," 5, citing Hasan's prose preface to his *divan*.

10. For Amīr Khusrow's biography, see Sunil Sharma, *Amir Khusraw: The Poet of Sufis and Sultans* (London: Oneworld, 2005).

11. Cited in Borah, "The Life and Works," 6. Translation modified.

12. *Fawā'id al-fu'ād*, ed. Tawfīq Subḥānī (Tehran: Zuvvār, 1385/2006); translated into English by K. A. Nizami and Bruce Lawrence, *Nizam al-Din Awliya: Morals for the Heart: Conversations of Shaykh Nizam ad-din Awliya Recorded by Amir Hasan Sijzi* (New York: Paulist Press, 1992).

13. For an important discussion of the conflict in authority between the spiritual power of the Sufi *shaykh* and the sultanate in Delhi, see Simon Digby, "The Sufi Shaykh and the Sultan: A Conflict of Claims to Authority in Medieval India," *Iran* 28 (1990): 71–81.

14. 'Abd al-Qādir ibn Mulūk Shāh Badā'ūnī, *Muntakhab al-tawārīkh* (Lucknow, 1284/1868), 1:201, 262. The motives and consequences of the move to Dawlatabad have been debated for centuries. The accounts of Ibn Battuta and Barani are now regarded as exaggerated in their negativity. For modern scholarly views, see Carl Ernst, *Eternal Garden: Mysticism, History, and Politics at a South Asian Sufi Center* (Albany: SUNY Press, 1992), 111–13; and K. A. Nizami, *State and Culture in Medieval India* (Delhi: South Asia Books, 1985), 116.

15. 'Abd al-Raḥmān Chishtī, *Mir'at al-Asrar*, held in British Library MS. Or. 216 (cited in Borah, "The Life and Works," 3). For a discussion of this text and its author, see Muzaffar Alam, "The Mughals, the Sufi Shaikhs, and the Formation of the Akbari Dispensation," *Modern Asian Studies* 43, no. 1 (2009): 142, with further references at note 15.

16. For Amīr Khusrow's use of Indian languages, see his *Nuh sipihr*, ed. Mohammad Wahid Mirza (London: Oxford University Press, 1950), 147–201.

17. For more on the *'Ishqnāma*, see Rebecca Gould, "Persian Love in an Indian Environment: Ḥasan Sijzī's Metaphysics of Sexual Desire," in *Beloved: Love and Languishing in Middle Eastern Literatures and Cultures: A Volume of Essays*, ed. Michael Beard, Alireza Korangy, and Hanadi al-Samman (London: I. B. Tauris, 2015).

18. Major studies of this literary device include Paul Losensky, "Linguistic and Rhetorical Aspects of the Signature Verse (*takhalluṣ*) in the Persian Ghazal," *Edebiyat* 8 (1997): 239–71; and J. T. P. de Bruijn, "The Name of the Poet in Persian Poetry," in *Proceedings of the Third European Conference of Iranian Studies, Pt. 2: Mediaeval and Modern Persian Studies*, ed. Charles Melville (Wiesbaden: Reichert Verlag, 1999), 45–56.

19. Franklin Lewis, "Reading, Writing, and Recitation: Sanā'ī and the Origins of the Persian Ghazal" (Ph.D. diss., University of Chicago, 1995), 98.

20. For a more extended engagement with Khāqānī, this time in the form of a *qaṣīda* rather than a *ghazal*, see *Dīvān-i Amīr Ḥasan Sijzī Dihlavī*, ed. Nargis Jahān (Delhi: Intishārāt-i Ḥasrat Mūhānī Fā'undīshan, 2004), 611. For the reception of Khāqānī in Indo-Persian poetry generally, see Rebecca Gould, "The Geographies of 'Ajam: The Circulation of Persian Poetry from South Asia to the Caucasus," *Medieval History Journal* 18, no. 1 (2015): 87–119.

21. Hammer-Purgstall's translation is discussed in Shafiq Shamel, "Persian Ear Rings and 'Fragments of a Vessel': Transformation and Fidelity in Hammer-Purgstall's Translation of Two Ghazals by Hafiz," *Monatshefte* 102, no. 1 (2010): 31.

22. For the Laylī and Majnūn story in Persian literature, see Ali Asghar Seyed-Gohrab, *Laylī and Majnūn: Love, Madness, and Mystic Longing in Niẓāmī's Epic Romance* (Leiden: Brill, 2003); and Iu. I. Krachkovskii, *Izbrannye sochineniia* (Moscow: AN SSSR, 1960), 2:588–632, available in Persian translation in *Laylī va Majnūn: pazhūhishī dar rīshah'hā-yi tārīkhī va ijtimā'ī-i dāstān: bih inẓimām-i talkhīṣ va sharḥ-i Laylī va Majnūn-i Niẓāmī* (Tehran: Zavvār, 1997).

23. W. H. Auden, "Writing [1932]," in *The English Auden: Poems, Essays, and Dramatic Writings, 1927–1939*, ed. Edward Mendelsohn (London: Random House, 1977), 308.

24. Alessandro Bausani, "The Development of Form in Persian Lyrics: A Way to a Better Understanding of the Structure of Western Poetry," *East and West* 9 (1958): 150.

25. As the translation I have given of two of these *radīfs—gūyīm* and *nimīpursīm*—indicates, classical Persian poets often use the first person plural to signify the first person singular; I have tended to translate these plural usages by singular verbs.

26. These ideas are explored in greater detail in Rebecca Gould, "Inimitability versus Translatability: The Structure of Literary Meaning in Arabo-Persian Poetics," *Translator* 19, no. 1: 81–104.

27. Walter Benjamin, "Die Aufgabe des Übersetzers," in *Gesammelte Schriften*, ed. Rolf Tiedemann and Hermann Schweppenhäuser (Frankfurt am Main: Suhrkamp Verlag, 1972–89), 4:20.

28. Walter Benjamin, "Die Aufgabe des Übersetzers," 4:10. Translation mine.

29. For this quotation, see Bausani, "The Development of Form in Persian Lyrics," 152. For the *ghazal* from the vantage point of world literature, see the volumes edited by Thomas Bauer and Angelika Neuwirth, *Ghazal as World Literature* (Beirut: Orient-Institut, 2005).

30. See Salomatshoeva's introduction to Hasan's *dīwān*, 19.

31. Mario Casari, "INDIA xiv. Persian Literature in India," in *Encyclopedia Iranica,* vol. 13, fasc. 1 (Costa Mesa, Calif.: Mazda Publishers, 1991–), 48–53.

32. Walter Benjamin, "Die Aufgabe des Übersetzers," 4:14.

33. Bernard Cerquiglini's *Eloge de la variante: Histoire critique de la philologie* (Paris: Seuil, 1989) usefully reflects on the philological specificities of premodern manuscript culture in terms that speak to Persian manuscript culture.

34. Two editions of Hasan's poetry were published in the same year: *Dīvān-i Ḥasan Sijzī Dihlavī: sadah-i haftum va hashtum,* ed. Aḥmad Bihishtī Shīrāzī and Ḥamīd Riẓā Qilīch Khānī (Tehran: Anjuman-i Āṣār va Mafākhir-i Farhangī, 2004); and *Dīvān-i Amīr Ḥasan Sijzī Dihlavī,* ed. Nargīs Jahān (Delhi, 2004). While both editions list manuscripts variants, the Tehran edition is based on a wider assortment of manuscripts and contains fewer errors. I have therefore preferred the readings in the Tehran edition over those in the Delhi edition.

35. I refer to the numbering in the Tehran edition, which conveniently numbers the entire corpus of Hasan's *ghazals*. The Delhi edition numbers the *ghazals* according to the *ravī* rather than cumulatively.

36. Geoffrey Squires, *Hafez: Translations and Interpretations of the Ghazals* (Miami, Oh.: Miami University Press, 2014).

After Tomorrow the Days Disappear

Ghazals

GHAZAL 1

Since my lover parted two days have passed.
Every joy left this body when he parted.
Like a bird torn from its nest, I lament
separation from my beloved's door.
When life was severed from the body,
it became impossible to part from the beloved's door.
Observe the city, killed by the arrow of my lover's glance:
Signs of parting puncture the arrow's tips.
Time yearns for blood, while the grief
of my beloved's departure is killed by stars.
Since it is my fate to be killed by grief,
I am severed from sorrow, stars, and time.
Observe Hasan: far from his beloved,
unaware of his heart, far from home.

radīf: judā [جدا]
(separated)

GHAZAL 2

If the lover does not hold the beloved's hand
when the beloved is in pain, there's no use for a doctor.
My pain has crossed the limits of endurance.
Oh, slave! Arise, and seek a doctor's note.
Oh, soul, what are the alms of beauty to me?
Or is my misfortune never to receive alms?
Send to me a charm inscribed with sorcery
so that I can bind my rivals' eyes in the city.
If you go to the temple of faiths in the Friday mosque,
you'll find a hundred errors in the preacher's speech.
For the heart that lingers by your door, paradise is only there.
Strangers don't reside in that person's city.
Without you, Hasan will find no homeland for his heart.
Without a flower the world is desolate for the nightingale.

radīf: rā [را]
(accusative case marker)

Hey you, proud like a new moon, increasing a festival's bounty,
your ruby opens the door of conquest and acceptance.
If the new moon hides behind a veil, then remove the veil from its
    face.
Since the crescent of your brows frames the festivity, it is flawless.
You say that you have seen me for a month. Your claim is justified.
Given this case, you should draw a firm message from this musk.
The collar of desire was pulled out of the neck when the discovery
of your love was made. Who will enjoy its imitation?
By God, no idol enjoyed love's dominion.
You are the authority on God's unity among the seekers.
Oh, preacher, you have endowed every sermon with brevity.
Observe the redundancy today of ten eulogies.
One who drinks to courage ignores both worlds.
Hasan! If you want a friend, step forward, away from solitude.

radīf: rā [را]
(accusative case marker)

GHAZAL 4

Cypress, pulling up the moonlight,
in jest you decorate the moon with a crooked hat.
You steal our heart by means of your high stature.
Oh, reformed friend, why do you bring along a witness?
The sun-worshippers said: we are the slaves
of the two sides of the sun's face.
Their beauty resembles the moon.
Your face is complete in all qualities like the moon.
The inscribed black letters fill the surroundings of the moon.
Hasan the slave writes in his beautiful way.
Wherever his writing is on display, the king will be its patron.

radīf: rā [راً]
(accusative case marker)

GHAZAL 5

Your face is the moon of our assembly.
Without your love, our hearts are empty.
We purchased your love by selling our souls.
This love is the sole outcome of our lives.
As our goals fill your alley,
We have no need for blessings or immortality.
The moon is shameless in the presence of your face.
The evening opposes us.
Poor Hasan utters to you secretly—
now the assassin's identity is known.

radīf: *mā* [ما]
(our)

Amid this grief, of what use is luxury?
Given what I have from you, of what use are remedies?
Oh, life! My soul is willing to sacrifice your love.
Since a lover lives only for his beloved, of what use is life?
Lovers do not strut in front of you.
What is a worldly garden compared to the bird of paradise?
When your lips strike the lover's eye,
they are given immortal life.
Of what use are the reports of the fountain of life?
Everyone who meets you reaches his desire.
Of what use is rain to a crop that is ripe?
Oh, rival, why do you linger at the gate?
Of what use are gatekeepers to the doors of the sky?
Hasan's resting place is the door of your peace.
Of what use is hoping for return after reaching your door?

radīf: che hājat ast [چه حاجت است]
(what is the use?)

Oh, heart, all inhabitants living by his fortune seek Him.
What is the use of this society? Instead seek Him,
the true distraction. If you want a balm for your affliction,
then seek the heart of the refined and heartsick ones.
Oh, love, you know he is yours. Show some intimacy!
You abuse reason and faith. Seek your own lover!
One arrow from the religion of saints is sweeter than a hundred of you.
Give up the religion of imitation. Seek those with right belief.
Open yourself to those arrayed in good fortune.
Hasan, instead of seeking fortune, try seeking Him.

radīf: *ṭalab* [طلب]
(she/he seeks)

What have you done, my God, with me and my fate?
Four days of separation means a month of fourteen evenings.
I will elucidate how the moon becomes moony.
A moon peeps through in the morning, but its epithet is the sun.
Regarding myself, wine, my beloved, ecstasy, and my intoxicated love,
you know how it is: the sadness of faith and renunciation that follows.
It has been said that I have patience, purity, and goodness.
Bring the bowl of wine and don't seek lies from me.
Hasan, in this matter you have no rivals.
Harness a rein of affection toward courtesy.

Friends, today in my head, desire is something else.
The flower of hope smells for me of another's loyalty.
I have found another light in the morning breeze.
In the dawn of truthful appearances, the breeze is something else.
Oh, tender heart, terrified of surrendering life.
Dying in the presence of the beloved is survival of another kind.
We do not speak of those who know reality.
For the bird of that garden, even this flute is something else.
I am a fire temple burning in the light of this truth.
The view of the beloved is something else.
The locks of her musky hair have clasped my heart.
Her locked coils bring trouble of a different order.
Oh, Hasan, how often do you circle the beloved's coils?
This movement toward the beloved is something else.

radīf: *digarast* [دگر است]
(is something else)

Saqi, the night is long.
Bring me wine while hope lingers.
We see your face and prostrate.
This is how we pray in our religion.
When Mahmud desired the *Book of Kings*
he was a lover of Ayyaz.
I am ready to unite with you.
This work is in someone's reliable hand.
You are not proud of my appearance.
Your face shelters my humility.
Your hair and face will accompany me.
The candle is lit. The night is long.
While your style is based on boasting,
Hasan makes do with thinking.

radīf: *ast* [است]
(is)

Who makes the sapling in the garden bloom?
Who makes the flower green in the garden?
Oh, Lord, send me an astronomer.
From what sky does the sun, wandering in the evening, come?
My heart bled from the flirtation of the lover's brows.
I recognize these arrows, and I know by whose bow they were
    sent.
I know that a thousand have been killed with these eyes,
but I don't know whose spring of life that is, and whose soul
    brings it.
Oh, wind, you are a fresh lily's message.
Otherwise, how could you produce such delicacy?
When the sky saw the verses of Hasan, it said to Time:
I see a stranger's dress. I wonder whose shop sells them.

radif: kist [کیست]
(who is?)

You are my only lover beneath the skies.
Nothing is dearer to me than this grief.
My lover's skirt is a flower: her tears are tulips and eyelashes
    clouds.
Our lover is no less than a new spring.
Every day I will comb the dust of your street.
No night has passed for me without anxiety.
The branch of union will bear fruit, I reasoned,
when a voice behind the door said there is no fruit.
Your voice then instructed me
to take up residence in another's street.
The pact between you and me
made no stipulation for a separate peace.
I would raise up the porch of my desire until it reaches the sky,
but my life's foundation is uncertain.
Either your pride is greater or Hasan's cry.
In both cases, measurements lie.

radif: *nīst* [نیست]
(is not)

The heart that does not yearn to burn
is not lightened by a beloved's intimacy.
Do not ask for competence or patience.
What I had yesterday is gone today.
Coquetry shatters souls.
Prudence in this battle brings defeat.
The ruthless Turk has no arrow
that does not pierce livers.
Uncooked heart! Burn on this love.
Anyone who does not yearn to burn is crude.
What do you know about the prosody of love?
Like a Qur'an, love does not teach tyranny.
Hasan! Do not boast of the morning of union.
Your night bears no trace of daylight's lucidity.

radīf: nīst [نیست]
(is not)

You think your face is a moon. So it is said, but it is untrue.
You think your hair smells of musk. So it is said, but it is untrue.
For the lovers, you named your face paradise, it is said,
while combing on jasmine and hyacinth. It is untrue.
Your hair is the injustice of oppression, a haven full of problems.
Your face is the light of Muslims, it is said. It is untrue.
If I tell you that your heart is sweet, that is true,
but when you say that I am difficult, that is untrue.
Oh, my love, the water of life is found in the earth near your door.
The second Alexander, it is said, has found the water of life. It is
    untrue.
I see Shah ʿAlā al-Dīn bestowing lifesaving grace
on anyone who pleads for life. It is untrue.
A shah served by one hundred servants
is like a *khaqan* and known as God. This is true.
The servant in front of you
is like a hundred *khaqan*s. This is untrue.

radīf: ke mīgūyad ke nīst [که می‌گوید که نیست]
("that which has been said is not true")

My writing viewed anguish as a mark of fidelity and left.
It accepted a great path, submitted, and left.
My lover took the locks of hair and spread them over me.
Why must one accept such strife for theft?
Many hearts like mine were stitched at that moment to my
    lover's eye.
My lover held the arrow of coquetry and left.
Oh, idol, you are the one whose heart is united with duplicity.
Attaining peace within your breast, you moved on.
I wish the stupidity in my head and with you
would come and settle and remain thus.
You caught me by force. Show kindness to me.
Hasan's tender heart has been taken by your hair.
Either bind me with a chain or let it pass.

radīf: gereft o gozhāsht [گرفت و گذاشت]
(taken and left)

The universe has no one to be one with.
Out of hundreds of watchers, not one can see.
From top to bottom, time's tree is thornless.
You search for a flower it doesn't have.
The world circulates good news
from man to man, promising what it doesn't have.
If someone sells vinegar on this street,
don't be angry that he doesn't offer sweets.
Someone who passed through the seven roofs of heaven
moved to the eight-gated garden without finding refuge there.
Hasan, why are you not mindful here?
After tomorrow the days disappear.

radīf: *nadārad* [ندارد]
(doesn't have)

The flower's petal is moistened by rain.
The branch's spine is bent by the wind.
Oh, bird! What creates each morning's loud lament?
Or does it cry from despair?
Look at the garden, beautiful inside and out.
I too have times of rejoicing.
Although there is a turtledove on the roof today,
its voice and rhythm constantly make sounds.
Oh, Saqi! Arise and pour the wine.
Hasan is not up to this feast.
His heart is free from the world's pains.
His peace exceeds the world's grief.
The Ka'ba of faith—greatness of the world—
holds in its palm the water of Zamzam.

radīf: *mīdārad* [می‌دارد]
(has)

Our inebriation intensifies when faced by your eyes.
Your temperament stems from Him whose existence has no end.
The smoke from my heart draws a tent over the cosmos, yes.
My love is a fire that does not turn back.
Love entered the world clinging to the lasso of your hair.
The heart with feet chained does not move.
Until I sip from your wine-colored lips,
my lust for worshipping wine can never pass.
You ask me, Hasan, why of drinking I don't repent.
By Allah, were I to repent, my drunkenness would never pass.

radīf: nimīravad [نمی‌رود]
(does not pass)

My fate lies between good fortune, morning time, and my lover.
The bringer of morning brings light to my eyes.
My wishes are fulfilled with less searching.
My lover rises with a little waiting.
His fresh moustache conquers the cosmos.
Colored by evening, his mole deceives fate.
Oh, God! What is that assembly like in paradise?
Kawthar flows through the tuba tree on the bank.
One of my hands holds a cup of wine
while the other clasps my lover's black locks.
No one searched for the drunkards.
The policemen were enraged after getting drunk.
Others leave behind gold and silver reserves.
Hasan leaves behind descriptions of his lover.

Hey! My grief at parting from you is more painful.
Being without you is harder than any other feat.
When you left me, I was afflicted for years by the skies.
This affliction is worse than the day of our separation.
Every night I cry, longing to unite with you.
Meanwhile your lament decreases daily.
When will a flower arrive from the garden of your union?
A fate less barren than the acacia thorn?
Your hair has entangled me.
The coils you possess ruthlessly distract my work.
I settle for the spring rain that boils in the vicinity
of your ruby lips. Each pearly drop is heavy.
Hey! Hasan's eyes have turned bloody from love of your rubies.
Either his eyes are filled with blood or your ruby lips are
    bloodthirsty.

Although we aged, the passion of youth never came.
Life departed. The beloved's form stayed.
I look within to see whether I have acquired more or less.
My patience is less. My love for idols is more.
Every evening the gardener locks the garden.
The bird rivals the flower until the sun dawns.
Although the enemy has been struck by Hasan's blade,
the culprit is outside and the beloved stands at the door.

Don't move from the place where you are since I can't leave you.
I am a slave to your face. Don't think of another one.
Whoever looks at your face sees vegetation and flowers.
The people of paradise need nothing else.
Aside from your grief, no one's sorrow is in my heart.
Aside from love of you, there is no chaos in the city.
On the evening of the market day, when your locks remain with me,
no profit can be extracted from trading with others.
If you throw Hasan's hope into the earth one hundred times,
he'll cast away the earth, and everything, except his desire for you.

radīf: digār [دگر]
(another/other)

Don't ask how drunk I am from the wine of separation.
One can stay away from a friend, but the distance should not be
　　long.
Where is holy Delhi and its beautiful mistresses?
It is a paradise, filled with beautiful women inside and outside its
　　walls.
What deceit! A wound festers on the vein of life.
Is there any escape when the leg of an elephant crushes the head of
　　an ant?
Although He manifests Himself through images,
for those who toil, His presence comes from searching.
Although your ruined memories have crossed the boundaries,
there is an inner space where I engage with your memory.
I have died a thousand deaths from the pain of your parting.
Still, the hope of union with you makes me patient.
Making love is hard between you and me, Hasan,
as hard as the union of the eye with the light it sees.

Without you, forgotten is my faith.
Forgotten are our proximities and intimacies.
I said to myself that I would hold your sorrow in my pocket.
Then my hands sank in the sleeves.
If Solomon saw your ruby lips,
by God, he'd forget his precious ring.
The worldly ones have forgotten hyacinth and jasmine
in the presence of your clothes and hair.
I say, if speech is unable to get across,
this is due to the beloved's presence.
Stirred by the regret of losing your beauty,
Hasan has lost his heart and forgotten faith and intellect.

radīf: farāmūsh [فراموش]
(forgotten)

My beloved stripped life from me. Farewell.
Life with my beloved is better than life itself. Farewell.
Jasmine parted from the jasmine garden. Goodbye.
Oh, garden, the flower is on a journey. Farewell.
An Egyptian caravan took Yusuf away.
Farewell, old man of Canaan, farewell.
The seal was stamped by fate.
A demon stole it. Oh, Solomon, farewell.
The lines of age were wiped from the tablet of my soul.
Dear neighbors of my childhood, farewell!
The silence has sealed my lips.
Oh, orators of the world, farewell!
My friends have left with their legs in stirrups.
Oh, Hasan, give me a hand, now! Farewell!

radīf: al-widāʿ [الوداع]
("farewell" in Arabic)

My work cost me my life. Such is the work of love.
Although I was killed, I could not escape love's elixir.
The lover of beautiful beings has spoiled my fate.
Dear Lord, the fate of love could not be worse than this!
The camel of the heart that has not pulled the load of love
will never arrive at his goal, will never reach home.
I have tears like tulips and my face is a jaundiced flower.
Yes, this is the sapling's blossom in love's spring.
Oh, Hasan, how long will you lust for flowers and gardens?
You should seek a thorn, since your path is strewn with love's
    thorns.

radīf: 'ishq [عشق]
(desire, love)

Hey! The world has given you its entire heart,
from the hand of parting to the end of living.
If your heart is not hewn from granite,
how do you behave with your slave?
You seek my heart although it bleeds.
I'll yield to my heart through my eyes.
One day you closed the middle of your hair.
The core of my heart drowned inside your locks.
Look how pleasing knowledge is to those
who have taken abode within your hair.
If my hand extends, I'll rein in my heart.
Its attraction to your beautiful hair will cease.
Oh, friend from of old, heed Hasan's tale
of woe, you kind-hearted soul.

radīf: del [دل]
(heart)

Let's follow the caravan to the different stations
in order to reach them. Farewell to our loved ones.
An evening of quiet passion makes everyone go insane.
Camels lift the unbound covenant.
This has remained from the sifting of days.
This has remained from the hope of union.
I could not prostrate when I parted.
My *qibla* disappeared from my side.
Hasan, you move planets of tears.
The moon cannot find its way home.

What is it? You don't even ask me once.
You don't ask my sorrow and desolation.
A true friend asks after his friend.
Oh, friend, why don't you ask about me?
I delight in dying from the pain of parting from you.
Reality abounds. My patience diminishes
while you ignore the nuances of more or less.
Last year, you received news of my despair.
Now, you ignore my sorrow.
The blood of Hasan became water, but he did not complain.
Oh, bloodthirsty idol, why didn't you ask about my pain?

radīf: *nimīpursīm* [داسَتم]
(you don't ask me)

Your arrangement and pact was what I didn't know.
Your kindness was vengeance. I didn't know.
Your speech, like your heart, was spoken harshly.
I didn't know that your heart was so rude.
Since I gave away my heart and flowery soul to Allah
I didn't know that it was part of this strategy.
I want to pull the bow of uniting with you.
I didn't know that our separation was hidden in ambush.
The heart surmised and understood the resurrection after death.
There was no doubt in me. It was a certainty. I didn't know.
I inhaled the breath of death on the morning of truth.
I didn't know that it was life's last breath.
Hasan gave his heart to you. You took his faith away.
It's true! Your heart planned this. I didn't know.

radīf: *bud man nadānestam* [بود، من ندانستم]
(I didn't know [that it was])

I only just learned of the anger and pride ingrained in you.
I only now understood your joke's form, within and without.
Your message was tied to my head.
Proximity to you augurs badly. This I knew.
Severed from you, my belt was the chain of separation.
I was unaware of this suffering. Now I know.
Among all entities, you possess the best qualities.
Your stature is an *alif* (ا). Your brow is the letter *nun* (ن).
In every heart is a city seething with love's fire.
I knew the desire to leave home.
I kissed your hair and remembered your ruby lips.
Yes, why should I fear the serpent, since I know a magic spell?
Oh, Hasan, having given your heart and faith to the idols,
examine the content of your brain for the key to your frenzied love.

radīf: *dānestam* [دانستم]
(I knew)

Immersed in sadness for you,
I didn't see the sun rise this year.
Only vanity made the divination of my heart sweet.
I didn't know that the divination was deceit.
Your flirting looted many hearts.
I knew you were a Turk but not that you were a killer too.
Although your ruby lips spoiled Hasan's work,
I knew nothing of this neglect.

radīf: *nimīdānistam* [نمی‌دانستم]
(I didn't know)

Come here! I am severed from my self when you are gone.
Make me happy with your return, so that my life can move.
You linger like Yusuf in the Egypt of beauty.
You cause me to leave the House of Sorrow.
Your lips leave me speechless again.
Although two feasts have passed since our parting, my mouth is
    sealed.
Your face was a flower, but it was better than a garden.
I was a nightingale, but I left the garden.
Smiling tulips and roses set thorns to my love.
I left with an ashen heart and soiled clothes.
You gave eloquence to my speech.
It's true: I have pursued the speech belonging to you.
Your city depends on Hasan's residence.
Hasan has left, but I am still within and soon must leave.

radīf: raftam [رفتم]
(I went)

I saw a figure the color of the night inscribed on the moon.
I saw the goal of the heart, and the favor of God.
It is said that the evening before the revelation of the Qur'an
is hidden during the year. I saw that auspicious evening in a month.
What qualities can I discern on that face and the lines inscribed
    there?
I saw a morning mixed with night.
All in one place, I saw her cheek, chin, and hair.
I saw Yusuf, the thread, and the well.
I saw friendship's morning light and the moonlit evening of
    pleasure.
I delighted in my lover's favor during inauspicious moments.
I saw one by one the forms my heart wishes for,
the kind instances of God's invisibility, unbound by words.
It spoke: ever since Hasan has glimpsed his beloved,
he has been oppressed by this sovereign face.

radīf: badīdam [بدیدم]
(I saw)

I write the tale of your longing.
The longer it grows, the longer my story grows.
My heart sheds fire. My lashes fill with water.
I don't know how to write this letter.
To describe my tears in wet eyes,
I write musings like hidden pearls.
If I knew that Laylī would read this letter,
why would I describe Majnūn's screams?
The inner chamber of my memory is the site for action.
The tale I write dwells on externalities.
The dark hues have disappeared from my eyes,
but I still inscribe this story in blood.
Hasan's *ghazals* are like this:
leading me to write charms for sorcerers.

radīf: *nevīsam* [بديدم]
(I wrote)

If one evening I stood on top of your mountain,
I would sing love. I would become your eternal companion.
I will migrate from my station every day
to reach your door where I will pass my days.
Since you are a specter, I must pray.
I will skip my prayer and prostrate instead to you.
How will selling my speech seem to you?
Yes, for the sword's sake I will make a scabbard.
You have placed a seal of silence on your intoxicating lip.
Do I have the gall to speak in front of you?
Hasan! Among the Sufis I have a bad name.
Now I'll earn respect among the wine worshippers.

radīf: *konam* [کنم]
(I make/do)

Oh God, either I am seated in front of you or I dream.
You're my guest on this much-desired moonlit evening.
A heart driven by lust for your lips heads for the tavern.
I see the vault of your brow in the *mihrab*.
The world extracts pure wine from your wine-colored lips.
Since you reached me, I see that the wine bleeds.
Your eyeballs resemble dice ready to roll.
I wish I could lose this game, but a hook keeps me stuck.
Your brows are a bow. Your lashes are flint.
You're full of holes. I see you wish to kill your lovers.
This is what I see: Hasan cast beneath your feet.
Either his sacred fortune has won or I dream.

radīf: mībīnam [می‌بینم]
(I see)

I see your face is like a garden.
I see your scar amid the tulips.
Due to your ardor, two of my eyes become four.
Two gardens become eight gardens.
The partridges are affected by your conduct.
I see the habitude of partridge and crow.
My heart burns in your hair's fire.
I see the jewel of the evening's lamp.
You like to inhale my fragrance.
I see what happens to your nose.
Hey! The city has been bargained away.
I see that this is Hasan's joke.

radīf: *mībīnam* [می‌بینم]
(I see)

My heart is an open wound. I don't know
whom to tell about my heart's death.
No path leads to my beloved's home.
Afflicted as I am, whom do I tell?
They ask me about union.
I don't know these issues. Whom do I tell?
I wish to speak of my beloved's hair,
but a knot seals my tongue. Whom do I tell?
I wanted to embrace my beloved's waist,
but it slipped from me. Whom do I tell?
The story of that mouth has no limit.
It won't fit in my mouth. Whom do I tell?
The story promised to produce a remedy for Hasan.
I am helpless when faced with his beauty. Whom do I tell?

radīf: bā gūyīm [با که گویم]
(whom do I tell?)

Lacking the ruby of your lips, my eyes filled with secret pearls.
Pupil of the eye, cast your glance again.
Your brow is etched well, as carefully as the mole above.
Your brows form the letter *nun* (ن), and the mole above is its dot.
The doctors legislate that the sick ones suffer from pain.
I will surrender my soul in front of you if you reject this law.
Oh, Laylī, you drive your followers' camels toward the Kaʻba.
You see how the guardians of the shrine are crazier than Majnūn.
All the while, Hasan, I bring my eyes and heart in front of you.
My tears are redder than agate. My heart's disposition is a hidden
    door.

Today the moon, park, and flower garden face you.
For the New Year it is enough that a rose is spread in front of you.
Yesterday, when I went to the garden, no narcissus was left.
My widened eyes were astonished by your countenance.
The sun, called the candle of the sky, has given its name to you.
Moths without number, who are your lovers, congregate around you.
When creatures pass through your infidel locks, they get lost.
We belong to the true religion. We are Muslims, facing you.
Oh, flower of all hearts! Wear a fresh countenance.
We are birds in your garden, guests for a few days with you.
Oh, soul, seek a pleasant melody from Hasan,
the sweet nightingale who faces a smiling rose and you.

radīf: rūyī tū [روی تو]
(your face)

The sorrow of knowing you is an old friend.
My affection for you dates to antiquity.
For us, my age is a temporary lover.
The love of you is a friend marked by age.
If one evening you make happiness enter my door,
you multiply age-old joys.
I swallow freshly attained grief
along with the witnesses of our old story.
You bring anguish, while Hasan
is wrapped in ancient notions of fidelity.

radīf: dīrnīh [دیرینه]
(ancient/old)

You discovered greenery in the newly watered flower.
You have made the nightingales of love drunk and full of grief.
You think that today is tomorrow forever.
To keep your word, you kept deferring the days.
Do whatever you want. You are your own adversary.
We have rejoiced many times over what you did to us.
You spare and take our lives with lips and amorous glances.
I don't know how you justify your claims.
Hasan, replace your old clothes with the royal robe.
For this hour, you have discovered a new style.

radīf: *kardehāyī* [کردهای]
(you have done [something])

Oh, breeze! You roam around, bringing bloodshed to us.
You bring sulfur to our distracted eyes.
My friends keep me waiting till my eyes turn red.
Give me the letter if it came from my friend.
You pierced my blameless heart with the arrow of desire.
You brought these markings to my heart from the Turks of Khatay.
Today in our city the only chaos is
the crisis caused by your sweet garments.
In that school, where prayers are said,
oh, teacher, from where did you bring this idol to the mosque?
Oh, Solomon, look at those fairy faces, one by one.
After getting drunk you trampled an ant beneath your feet.
You cast a side glance in the direction of Hasan.
You have stricken his heart with another wound.

radīf: *avardehāyī* [آورده‌ای]
(you have brought [something])

Hey, you! Who is Hasan's king? Whose subservient slave are you?
You hold up our curtain. Whose confidant are you?
You are a large pearl that will crown someone's head.
Tall cypress tree, whose long life endowed you?
The two-week moon brings a chessboard.
Hey, you, who move beautifully, to whom does fourteen belong?
Hey, you, generous to slaves in the times of need.
You who fulfill our need, whose secret need are you?
Hasan has said that he is your slave in a hundred different ways.
Therefore, in your own language you should say: whose slave
    are you?

radīf: *kistī* [كيستى]
(who are you?)

You pay no attention to acts of sympathy.
You certainly never noticed my sympathy.
The doctor who cures your lovers has been named.
Still, you don't have a cure for this disease.
Every instant, you strike to kill me.
You have no other entanglement than me.
Although you burn my soul and heart,
you won't find a lover more passionate than me.
Oh, intellect! We know His love.
You have no business with this kind of love.
Oh, claimant! Your life is unlawful. You have a heart.
But when it comes to love, there is no sympathy.
Hasan! Do not open the shop of your pretension.
Some days, there is no seeking trade.

radīf: *nadārī* [نداری]
(you don't have)

Without you my liver is roasted, as you know.
My heart is a crazed ruin, as you know.
You're no friend if I must sit in the garden without you.
A friendless garden is a torment, as you know.
I wait hopefully for you. What else can I do?
Life rushes forward, as you know.
You should quench my thirst. Your lips made me burn.
My life thrives, thanks to water. You know this.
What do you mean by asking Hasan: who is your lover?
The answer is what you already know.

radīf: to ham midoni [تو هم می‌دانی]
(you also/already know)

GHAZAL 48

You brought the news: a youth lost his heart.
Your kindness brought him back to life.
The dog was once at your door.
Today, nothing remains except his bones.
If only half the soul can be kissed,
then let illness excuse the other half of the soul.
You are good fortune or a day of grace.
You did not become my lover randomly.
You remove the curtain so that people can
see the garden amid the remaining shrubbery.
The astrologer said: I have never seen
a planet like that in any sky.
He did not see your eyes rolling with vanity,
if they ever did roll at the threshold of your head.
Sometimes you pardon Hasan for glancing at your lip.
Will you remember Hasan or not?

You don't cure the suffering of my heart.
Nor are you faithful to your promises.
You don't notice my condition in the evening.
You don't think about the day of punishment.
You don't let me breathe as my heart wills.
You don't release me from captivity.
Why do you wound your friends?
Why do you give your enemy victory?
You tighten your belt to shed the blood of strangers.
Don't kill! Don't kill! Killing is a sin.
When driven by desire, I am manly.
Why do you oppress me?
Your only fault is that
you treat your friends unjustly.

radīf: *mīkonī* [می‌کنی]
(second person singular, present imperfect tense, of "to do")

You are the envy of every idol maker.
You are the moon's forehead and Jupiter's brow.
The moon shines when you move in the sky.
Your face is a moon on earth.
Your flattery is kind.
God almighty is also kind.
No one has been created like you,
equal to thousands of created beings.
Pass a sweet moment with the slave Hasan.
Sit down, since your rival is already sitting.

Quatrains

✦ *Rubāʿiyyat* ✦

RUBĀʿĪ 1

When the lover heard that you slipped away,
fresh wine flowed from his eyes at dawn.
From the veil of your eyes, a dining mat is spread.
By the needle of your brow, a dress of dream is sewn.

radīf: ab [آب]
(can mean "water," also a sound cluster)

RUBĀ'Ī 2

The pain of the beloved that pierces the heart is like no other.
Piety and virtue are signs of others.
To be engaged by the lover is work of a different kind.
Beyond prayer and fasting, this work is like no other.

radīf: *digar ast* [دگر است]
(is other, different)

Oh, beloved, after a month, your oppression is immense.
Through this village, the tale of your cruelty has passed.
You said you would come on Saturday. The month reached an end.
Since you made your promise, Wednesday also has passed.

radīf: begozasht [بگذشت]
(has passed)

My heart is a garden from that mouth's blossom.
Your curls on my chest are a hundred caresses.
The parrot of your lips cannot be criticized for defects.
No one can conquer your lock of hair, as dark as the crow.

RUBĀʿĪ 5

Reeds learn from rancid stalks to write.
Flowers learn to weave silk from paper threads.
I tell my heart to make magic from its eye.
Captive in my lover's coils, it learns to hunt snakes.

radīf: *amukht* [آموخت]
(learns)

RUBĀʿĪ 6

If your name is inscribed on the sky's notebook,
so too is your daily bread purified by the page of life.
Although Noah lived a thousand years,
some thousand years have passed with him inside the earth.

Arbitration is meaningless to a judge of love.
All of his rulings lack reason.
Ever since the judge heard our story,
sorrow has been my companion.

The heart found out that the wind of the soul arose at dawn. It
    means your smell.
It planned a walk in the garden. This is a glorious passage to home.
Sometimes spring drives me crazy. This implies your face.
The book of the soul is attached to the chain of your request.

Whenever I cry for you, my tears come out differently.
Sometimes they are only water. Other times they are bloody.
However I make love to you, my tears flow this way.
We observe these movements as they go.

radīf: ayad [آید]
(comes)

The world is happy due to the fortune of your king.
The rotations of the sky have fallen at your feet.
Since five prayers are prescribed into the turning of time,
may Islam be strengthened with your five rotations!

I got so drunk, I sat down without my self.
I have lost heart. This grieving heart has no self.
I have seen myself a thousand times without you.
A day will come when I will see you without my self.

radīf: bī khūd [بی‌خود]
(without self)

Today the morning breeze is moved by the feet of spring.
In the science of narration it is called repetition.
Sometimes with the sun it moves to the east.
Here, it brings news from the flower.

Humans are made of fire, water, wind, and earth.
I am better than fire, water, wind, and earth.
My soul is not composed of fire, water, wind, and earth.
Surrender the law of fire, water, wind, and earth.

These distant childhood memories are full of deceit.
Whatever is inscribed there is wrought by Him, the precious pearl.
Handwritten fragments fade in the presence of His face.
I too want to be free of what was written long ago.

Although the world sometimes fears Genghis Khan,
and Muhammad's lineage faces its end,
now a Muhammad, the world's sultan, has appeared,
and purified the world of Genghis Khan's breed.

The rose bloomed without a scent. What can I do?
Water does not flow from it. What can I do?
Yesterday, the rose's notebook filled with pages.
It does not have even a folio of its face. What can I do?

radīf: *nadārad che konam* [ندارد چه کنم]
(does not have, what should I do?)

Oh, Khusrow! Accept the path of grace.
Whatever I, the slave Hasan, speak
is a speech unlike Khusrow's speech.
This speech is what I speak.

radīf: *mīgūyīm* [می‌گویم]
(I/we say)

Fragments

✦ *Qiṭaʿāt* ✦

Facing the moon, you are the sun.
On the idol's lips, you are a sweet ruby.
Your eyebrows trace the shape of the prayer altar.
The heart wreaks destruction in the mosque.
While I abide in grief, sadness, and piercing looks,
you have wine, a harp, and beauty.
The soul of your lover is lost in your tresses.
Search them and you may find it.
After all, what made me do that?
Between me and you, there is always pain.
God forbid that any fault come from you.
You are always true.
Beloved, it is not only I who love you.
Shaykhs and old men love you, too.
Your eyes are seeking plunder.
Yet you want mercy and oblation.
Don't entrust my heart to bloodthirsty eyes.
Sit down. Stay away from rebellion's way.

King of kings, ruler of the era,
may you protect the faithful ones. Amen.
Your domain stretches from east to west.
May your name be inscribed on every petition. Amen.
May the world have Yusuf's fortune in your gaze.
May it resemble feasting and laughter. Amen.
May joy always be blessed
with the gaze of Khiẓr Khān. Amen.
May the eminence of your princes always rise.
May the wheels of their fortune ascend. Amen!

radīf: *amin* [آمین]
(amen)

Ode

✦ *Qaṣīda* ✦

QAṢĪDA

When the hand of the sky moved the pawn of dawn.
An honest soul prayed for the king's fortune.
Shah of the world, 'Ala al-Din, protector of the true faith.
May the purity of God shelter the Shah, who shelters faith.
The feast arrived. Gifts were offered to moonlike beauty.
The Shah's abundant fortune is welcomed.

Ghazals

Ghazal 9   Compare *rubāʿī* 2 with the same *radīf.*

Ghazal 10   *saqi*: Cup-bearer or wine server at royal banquets, usually a young boy, frequently addressed in *ghazals.*

Ghazal 14   *khaqan*: A title assigned to medieval Mongol, Turkic, and Chinese rulers in classical Persian literary texts. Equivalent to the status of emperor or king of kings.

Ghazal 14   In the fourth *bayt* (lines 7–8), the *radīf* of this *ghazal* is intriguingly reversed, such that "it is said that it is" (که می گوید که هست) is counterpoised to "it is said that it is not" (که می گوید که نیست). This contrast underscores the metaphysical dimensions of Hasan's poetics.

Ghazal 17   *Zamzam*: A well located within the Masjid al-Haram (protected mosque) in Mecca, east of the Kaʿba. According to Islamic belief, this is the source of water that began to flow miraculously when Ismāʿīl (Ishmael), the infant son of Ibrāhīm (Abraham), thirsted; it is currently a pilgrimage site. Note that in this closing verse, when Hasan refers to the Kaʿba as the "greatness" of the world, he is also referring to his own formal name, Amīr Ḥasan pesar-i ʿAlāʾ, so "Kaʿba of faith" could also be rendered as "Kaʿba of the faith of ʿAlāʾ [=Ḥasan]."

Ghazal 19   fresh moustache: *khaṭṭ-i sabz* literally translates as "green line," the moustache that appears on the face of an adolescent male before the appearance of his facial hair.

Ghazal 19   Kawthar: Literally "abundance" in Arabic; a river in paradise. Al-Kawthar is also the name for chapter (*sūra*) 108, the shortest *sūra* of the Qurʾan.

Ghazal 19   tuba: Literally "blessedness" in Arabic; the tree that, according to Islamic tradition, grows in paradise (*jannah*); a symbol of abundance. According to the *Ṣaḥīḥ* of al-Bukhārī (4:474), the gowns of righteous dwellers of heaven are made from the fiber of the tuba tree's blossoms.

Ghazal 24   Solomon: The Qur'an regards King Solomon (Suleiman), the third king of Israel, as a prophet whose reign was blessed by God. In Persian poetry, he symbolizes just governance.

Ghazal 25   Yusuf: The biblical Joseph, who was sold into slavery by his brothers, and who by the end of his life had risen to a high position of power in the Egyptian administration. An entire chapter from the Qur'an (*sūra* 12) is dedicated to Yusuf's story. The narrative was subsequently incorporated into the Persian tradition, most notably by 'Abd al-Raḥmān Jami (d. 1492).

Ghazal 25   old man of Canaan: Yusuf's father Jacob (Yaqub).

Ghazal 28   *qibla*: Direction Muslims face during prayer; facing Mecca.

Ghazal 33   Yusuf: See note to *ghazal* 25, above.

Ghazal 34   "on the evening before the revelation / of the Qur'an": The Persian term here is *shab-i qadr* (literally "night of destiny"), which corresponds to the Arabic *laylat al-qadr*. This is the day in the Islamic calendar when the first verses of the Qur'an were revealed to Muhammad. My translation reflects this meaning, which is not spelled out in the original Persian.

Ghazal 37   *mihrab*: Prayer niche facing in the direction of the *qibla*.

Ghazal 40   Laylī: Female protagonist in an Arabian love story made famous by Niẓāmī of Ganja. The story of Laylī and Majnūn was a popular subject for literary composition by Persian and Indo-Persian poets.

Other Poems

Rubā'ī 2   Compare *ghazal* 9 with the same *radīf*.

Rubā'ī 3   "your cruelty has passed": I prefer here the manuscript variant جفا (cruelty) over وفا (loyalty), printed in the Tehran edition.

Rubā'ī 12   "science of narration": Hasan uses the term *'ilm-i hadith*, which refers to the discipline of gathering and refining sayings associated with the Prophet and his companions. However, *hadith* also means "story" or "event," so it is possible to translate the phrase here as "the science of narration."

Rubā'ī 13   "Fire, water, wind, and earth": The four elements, carried over from the Greek system into the Islamic sciences.

Rubāʿī 15   This *rubāʿī* is unusual in being marked by historical circumstance. While "Muhammad's stock [*al-i muhammad*]" simply means Muslims, "Sultan Muhammad" probably refers to Muhammad Tughluq of Delhi (r. 1325–51). This sultan was responsible for relocating the capital of the sultanate from Delhi to Dawlatabad, partly in order to protect his state against the Mongol invasions. Hasan was one among many residents of Delhi who was compelled to move south as a result of this violence.

Qiṭaʿ 2   Yusuf: See note to *ghazal 25*.

Qaṣīda

This *qaṣīda* has been included in this collection of Hasan's lyric verse in order to demonstrate that Hasan did deploy the panegyric idiom. The brevity of this poem stretches the very definition of *qaṣīda*, which is typically a lengthy poem.

padīshāh   A longer version of the regal title *shah*.

Editions Consulted

Dīvān-i Ḥasan Sijzī Dihlavī: sadah-i haftum va hashtum. Ed. Aḥmad Bihishtī
  Shīrāzī and Ḥamīd Riżā Qilīch Khānī. Tehran, 2004.
Dīvān-i Amīr Ḥasan Sijzī Dihlavī. Ed. Nargīs Jahān. Delhi, 2004.

Ghazals

T – Tehran Edition. *Ghazal* number, followed by page number in brackets.
D – Delhi Edition. Page number only; number not given because the num-
  bering is not consecutive and starts over with each section.
– Not found in that edition.

No.	T	D	Opening Verse (English)	Opening Verse (Persian)
1	4[2]	128	Since my lover parted, two days have passed.	دو روز شد که شدم زان مه یگانه جدا
			Every joy left this body when he parted.	همه نشاط شد از من، بدین بهانه جدا
2	6[5]	140	If the lover does not hold the beloved's hand	بر درد ما وقوف نباشد طبیب را
			when the beloved is in pain, there's no use for a doctor.	آه ار حبیب دست نگیرد حبیب را
3	12[8]	133-4	Hey, you, proud like a new moon, increasing a festival's bounty,	ای غرّهٔ چون ماه نو، رونق فزوده عید را
			your ruby opens the door of conquest and acceptance.	لعل تو بگشاده دری، هم فتح هم تأیید را
4	25[14]	119	Cypress, pulling up the moonlight,	ای برفراز سرو برآورده ماه را
			in jest you decorate the moon with a crooked hat.	بر ماه، کج نهاده به شوخی کلاه را

No.	T	D	Opening Verse (English)	Opening Verse (Persian)
5	37[19]	-	Your face is the moon of our assembly.	ای روی توماه مخفل ما
			Without your love, our hearts are empty.	جز عشق تو نیست در دل ما
6	67[33]	181	Amidst this grief, of what use is luxury?	اندر غم تو ام سر و سامانچه حاجستست
			Given what I have from you, of what use are remedies?	چون دردم از تو باشد درمان چه حاجستست
7	56[28]	145	Oh, heart, all inhabitants living by his fortune seek Him.	ای دل اهل دولت ایشانند، ایشان را طلب
			What is the use of this society? Instead seek Him	یست این جمعیت، آن جمع پریشان را طلب
8	55[28]	147	What have you done, my God, with me and my fate?	چه کرد با من و با روزگار من یارب
			Four days of separation means a month of fourteen evenings.	چهار روزه فراق مه چهارده شب
9	100[48]	186-7	Friends, today in my head, desire is something else.	دوستان در سرم امروز هوایی دگر است
			The flower of hope smells for me of another's loyalty.	گل امید مرا بوی وفایی دگر است
10	105[50]	-	Saqi, the night is long.	ساقی ما شب دارز است
			Bring me wine while hope lingers.	می ده که درامید باز است
11	156[75]	179	Who makes the sapling in the garden bloom?	باز این یکی نهال تو از بوستان کیست
			Who makes the flower green in the garden?	وان گل که سبزه می کند از گلستان کیست

No.	T	D	Opening Verse (English)	Opening Verse (Persian)
12	165[80]	160	You are my only lover beneath the skies.	ما را از بجز تو در همه آفاق یار نیست
			Nothing is dearer to me than this grief.	مشفق‌تر از غم تو دگر غمگسار نیست
13	167 [80–81]	188	The heart that does not yearn to burn	دل که در او چاشنی سوز نیست
			is not lightened by a beloved's intimacy.	محرم دلدار دل‌افروز نیست
14	179[86]	149-50	You think your face is a moon. So it is said, but it is untrue.	روی خود را ماه می‌خوانی که می‌گوید که نیست
			You think your hair smells of musk. So it is said, but it is untrue.	موی خود را مشک می‌دانی که می‌گوید که نیست
15	186[90]	185-6	My writing viewed anguish as a mark of fidelity and left.	نگار من که جفا را وفا گرفت و گذاشت
			It accepted a great path, submitted, and left.	رۀ تکبّر و رسم رضا گرفت و گذاشت
16	233[111]	258	The universe has no one to be one with.	فلک باکس دل یکتا ندارد
			Out of hundreds of watchers, not one can see.	ز صد دیده یکی بینا ندراد
17	238[113]	249	The flower's petal is moistened by rain.	روی گل از هوا نمی دارد
			The branch's spine is bent by the wind.	پشت شاخ از صبا خمی دارد
18	363[172]	320	Our inebriation intensifies when faced by your eyes.	از چشم پرخمار تو مستی نمی‌رود
			Your temperament stems from Him, whose existence has no end.	خویت از آن مزاج که هستی نمی‌رود

No.	T	D	Opening Verse (English)	Opening Verse (Persian)
19	410[194]	334	My fate lies between good fortune, morning time, and my lover.	بخت بین کامروز وقت صبح، یار
			The bringer of morning brings light to my eyes.	چشم روشن کرد ما را صبحوار
20	419[198]	342	Hey! My grief at parting from you is more painful.	ای مرا حال از غمت از هرچه دانی زارتر
			Being without you is harder than any other feat.	بی‌تو بودن از همه دشوارها دشوارتر
21	426[201]	343	Although we aged, the passion of youth never came.	پیر شدیم و نشد شور جوانی ز سر
			Life departed. The beloved's form stayed.	عمر برفت و نرفت صورت یار از نظر
22	429[202]	347	Don't move from the place where you are since I can't leave you.	مشو از جای که از تو نشدم جای دگر
			I am a slave to your face. Don't think of another one.	بندهٔ روی توآم تا نکنی رای دگر
23	431[203]	344	Don't ask how drunk I am from the wine of separation.	مپرس کز می فرقت چگونه‌ای مخمور
			One can stay away from a friend, but the distance should not be long.	ز دوست دور توان شد ولی نه چندان دور
24	474 [224–25]	365	Without you, forgotten is my faith.	ای بی تو مرا ز دین فراموش
			Forgotten are our proximities and intimacies.	وز همدم و همنشین فراموش

No.	T	D	Opening Verse (English)	Opening Verse (Persian)
25	477[224]	370	My beloved stripped life from me. Farewell.	دل ز ما برداشت جانان، الوداع
			Life with my beloved is better than life itself. Farewell.	جان بدو اولیٰتر از جان، الوداع
26	480[227]	373	My work cost me my life. Such is the work of love.	کارم به جان رسید همین است کار عشق
			Although I was killed, I could not escape love's elixir.	سر رفت و هم نمی‌رود از سر خمار عشق
27	489 [231–32]	378	Hey! The world has given you its entire heart,	ای داده به تو همه جهان دل
			from the hand of parting to the end of living.	از دست فِراق تو به جان دل
28	490[232]	380	Let's follow the caravan to the different stations	برانیم با کاروان یک دو منزل
			in order to reach them. Farewell to our loved ones.	وداع عزیزان، رسانیدن دل
29	500[237]	400	What is it? You don't even ask me once.	چیست که یکبار نمی‌پرسیَم
			You don't ask my sorrow and desolation.	زین غم و تیمار نمی‌پرسیَم
30	505[239]	388	Your arrangement and pact was what I didn't know.	قرار و عهد تو این بود، من ندانستم
			Your kindness was vengeance. I didn't know.	نوید مِهر تو کین بود، من ندانستم

No.	T	D	Opening Verse (English)	Opening Verse (Persian)
31	506[240]	435	I only just learned of the anger and pride ingrained in you.	خشم و نازی که ترا بود کنون دانستم
			I only now understood your joke's form, within and without.	شکل شوخی تو بیرون و درون دانستم
32	507[240]	435	Immersed in sadness for you,	من در اندوه تو این حال نمی‌دانستم
			I didn't see the sun rise this year.	اثر طالع این سال نمی‌دانستم
33	512[242]	388	Come here! I am severed from my self when you are gone.	بیا که تا تو برفتی ز خویشتن رفتم
			Make me happy with your return, so that my life can move.	مرا به آمدنت شاد کن که من رفتم
34	529[250]	440	I saw a figure the color of the night inscribed on the moon.	شبگون رقمی بر رخ آن ماه بدیدم
			I saw the goal of the heart, and the favor of God.	مقصود دل المنه‌لله بدیدم
35	553[261]	399	I write the tale of your longing.	حدیث اشتیاقت چون نویسم
			The longer it grows, the longer my story grows.	ز هر چ افزون‌تر است افزون نویسم
36	575[272]	427	If one evening I stood on top of your mountain,	اگر شبی به سر کوی تو مقام کنم
			I would sing love. I would become your eternal companion.	صلای عشق دهم، عشرت مدام کنم

No.	T	D	Opening Verse (English)	Opening Verse (Persian)
37	583[275]	429	Oh God, either I am seated in front of you or I dream.	منم یا رب نشسته پیش تو یا خواب می‌بینم
			You're my guest on this much-desired moonlit evening.	تو مهمان منی کامشب شب مهتاب می‌بینم
38	585[276]	440	I see your face is like a garden.	روی تو همچو باغ می بینم
			I see your scar amid the tulips.	لاله را از تو داغ می بینم
39	625[295]	387	My heart is an open wound. I don't know	دلِ خون شد، ندانم با که گویم
			whom to tell about my heart's death.	چه دل کز دل به جانم، با که گویم
40	688[324]	489	Lacking the ruby of your lips, my eyes filled with secret pearls.	بی‌لعل لبت پر شد، چشمم ز دُر مکنون
			Pupil of the eye, cast your glance again.	ای مردمک دیده، آخر نظری اکنون
41	720[339]	499	Today the moon, park, and flower garden face you.	امروز ماه و باغ و گلستان روی تو
			For the New Year it is enough that a rose is spread in front of you.	نوروز ما بس است گل افشان روی تو
42	746[350]	511	The sorrow of knowing you is an old friend.	ای غمت آشنای دیرینه
			My affection for you dates to antiquity.	با تو ما را هوای دیرینه
43	748[351]	-	You discovered greenery in the newly watered flower.	بزهٔ تر کز گل سیراب پیدا کرده‌ای
			You have made the nightingales of love drunk and full of grief.	بلبلان عشق را سرمست و شیدا کرده‌ای

No.	T	D	Opening Verse (English)	Opening Verse (Persian)
44	749[352]	-	Oh, breeze! You roam around, bringing bloodshed to us.	ای صبا گردی که زان خونریز ما آورده‌ای
			You bring sulfur to our distracted eyes.	چشم خون افشان ما را توتیا آورده‌ای
45	767[360]	-	Hey, you! Who is Hasan's king? Whose subservient slave are you?	ای تو به حسن پادشه بنده نواز کیستی
			You hold up our curtain. Whose confidant are you?	پردهٔ ما هم‌می‌دری محرم راز کیستی
46	787[369]	556	You pay no attention to acts of sympathy.	نظر بر هیچ غمخواری نداری
			You certainly never noticed my sympathy.	وگر داری، به من باری نداری
47	846[395]	538	Without you my liver is roasted, as you know.	جگرم بی کباب است تو هم می‌دانی
			My heart is a crazed ruin, as you know.	دل دیوانه خراب است تو هم می‌دانی
48	849[396]	-	You brought the news: a youth lost his heart.	خبر دادی که بی‌دل شد جوانی
			Your kindness brought him back to life.	به جان آمد ز مهرت مهربانی
49	861[401]	594	You don't cure the suffering of my heart.	نه درد دلم را دوا می‌کنی
			Nor are you faithful to your promises.	نه بر گفتهٔ خود وفا بکنی
50	865[403]	528	You are the envy of every idol maker.	تو رشک همه بتان چینی
			You are the moon's forehead and Jupiter's brow.	مه جبهه و مشتری جبینی

Other Poems

Rubāʿīs

No.	T	D	Opening Verse (English)	Opening Verse (Persian)
1	9[584]	821	When the lover heard that you slipped away,	از دیده همی‌ریخت سحرگه می ناب
			fresh wine flowed from his eyes at dawn.	از پردهٔ چشم خویش بهر سفرت
2	10[584]	822	The pain of the beloved that pierces the heart is like no other.	دل را غمِ یار خارخاری دگر است
			Piety and virtue are signs of others.	تقوی و صلاحیت شعاری دگراست
3	38[590]	822	Oh, beloved, after a month, your oppression is immense.	جانا ستم تو برکه و مه بگذشت
			Through this village, the tale of your cruelty has passed.	دستان وفای تو ازین ده بگذشت
4	14[585]	823	My heart is a garden from that mouth's blossom.	از غنچه آن دهن دل من باغ است
			Your curls on my chest are a hundred caresses.	وز زلف تو در سینهٔ من صد داغ است
5	28[588]	824	Reeds learn from rancid stalks to write.	سبزه ز خط ترش دبیری آموخت
			Flowers learn to weave silk from paper threads.	گل ز رخت اوراق حریری آموخت
6	15[585]	828	If your name is inscribed on the sky's notebook,	گر نام تو نقش دفتر افلاک است
			so too is your daily bread purified by the page of life.	هم از ورق حیات روزی پاک است

No.	T	D	Opening Verse (English)	Opening Verse (Persian)
7	25[587]	829	Arbitration is meaningless to a judge of love.	با قاضی عشق داوری بیهوده است
			All of his rulings lack reason.	کاو را همه حکمهای ناحق بوده است
8	-	829	The heart found out that the wind of the soul arose at dawn. It means your smell.	دل یافت نسیم جان فزا در شب گیر – یعنی بویت
			It planned a walk in the garden. This is a glorious passage to home.	کردست به رفتن گلستان تدبیر – یعنی کویست
9	56[593]	830	Whenever I cry for you, my tears come out differently.	هر دم ز تو اشک من دگرگون آید
			Sometimes they are only water. Other times they are bloody.	گاهی هم آب و گه همه خون آید
10	41[590]	831	The world is happy due to the fortune of your king.	ای جمله جهان به دولت ملک تو شاد
			The rotations of the sky have fallen at your feet.	نوبت نوبت فلک به پای تو فتاد
11	43[592]	832	I got so drunk, I sat down without my self.	چند از می غم مست نشینم بی‌خود
			I have lost heart. This grieving heart has no self.	من بی‌دل و این دل حزینم بی‌خود
12	60[594]	837	Today the morning breeze is moved by the feet of spring.	امروز صبا را ز قدم‌های بهار
			In the science of narration it is called repetition.	در علم حدیث بود گویی تکرار

No.	T	D	Opening Verse (English)	Opening Verse (Persian)
13	63[594]	838	Humans are made of fire, water, wind, and earth.	از آتش و آب و باد و خاک است بشر
			I am better than fire, water, wind, and earth.	من ز آتش و آب و باد و خاکم برتر
14	72[596]	841	These distant childhood memories are full of deceit.	آن دورنویس کودک پر تلبیس
			Whatever is inscribed there is wrought by Him, the precious pearl.	هرچند که نقش اوست چون دُرّ نفیس
15	-	844	Although the world sometimes fears Genghis Khan,	گر داشت گهی جهان ز چنگیز خان باک
			and Muhammad's lineage faces its end	تا آل محمد از پیش دید هلاک
16	87[599]	846	The rose bloomed without a scent. What can I do?	گل آمد و بوی او ندارد چه کنم
			Water does not flow from it. What can I do?	چون آب ز جوی او ندارد چه کنم
17	-	847	Oh, Khusrow! Accept the path of grace.	خسرو از راه احسان بپذیر
			Whatever I, the slave Hasan, speak	آنچه من بنده حسن می‌گویم

Qiṭaʿs and Qaṣīda

No.	T	D	Opening Verse (English)	Opening Verse (Persian)
Qiṭa 1	-	816	Facing the moon, you are the sun.	در روی مها چو آفتابی
			On the idol's lips, you are a sweet ruby.	در لب صنما چو لعل نابی
Qiṭa 2	13 [530]	807	King of kings, ruler of the era,	شهنشاه زمانه دولت تو
			may you protect the faithful ones. Amen.	امان اهل ایمان باد آمین
Qaṣīda 1	10 [432]	615	When the hand of the sky moved the pawn of dawn.	دست فلک چو بر کشد بیدق صبحگاه را
			An honest soul prayed for the king's fortune.	روح امین دعا کند دولت پادشاه را

1206   Establishment of the Delhi Sultanate by the Ghurid dynasty (originating in present-day Afghanistan).

1253   Birth of Hasan and of Amīr Khusrow.

1266   Ghiyath al-Din Balban, the sultan during the era in which *'Ishqnāma* is set, ascends the throne in Delhi.

1287   End of the reign of Ghiyath al-Din Balban; succeeded by the brief reign of Muiz al-Din Qayqubad (1287–90).

1290   End of the so-called Mamluk (alternatively, Ghulam or Slave) dynasty of Delhi; beginning of the Khilji dynasty with the reign of Jalal al-din Firuz Khilji.

1296   ʿAla al-Dīn Khilji, dedicatee of *Book of Desire* and Hasan's longest-standing patron, ascends the throne in Delhi.

1301   Hasan completes *Book of Desire* in one night (according to his testimony).

1314   Amīr Khusrow is requested by Prince Khizr Khan to compose the *masnavī Duwal Rani Khizr Khan*, concerning his ill-fated romance with a Hindu princess (Duwal Rani).

1316   Sultan ʿAla al-Dīn Khilji dies, poisoned by his general Malik Kafur; Shah Mubarak ascends the throne in Delhi; rules until 1320.

1318   Amīr Khusrow completes *Nuh Sipihr* (*Nine Heavens*), the first detailed account of Indian culture, customs, and languages in Persian.

1325   Niẓām al-Dīn and Amīr Khusrow die in Delhi; Muhammad Tughluq ascends the throne.

1327   Initial (voluntary) relocation of some subjects of the Delhi Sultanate to Dawlatabad (Deogir) by Muhammad Tughluq.

1329   Second (mandatory) relocation of all subjects of the Delhi Sultanate to Dawlatabad.

c. 1330   Hasan dies in Dawlatabad.

1351   End of the reign of Muhammad Tughluq.

Amīr Khusrow (1253–1325) Major Indo-Persian poet; friend of and mentor to Hasan; he and Hasan studied with the major Chishtī *shaykh* Nizām al-Dīn Awliya.

bayt ("tent" or "home") Couplet; two *misra's* (hemistiches) constitute one *bayt*.

Chishti Branch (*tariqa*) of Sufism that took particularly deep root in South Asia. The most famous practitioner of this *tariqa* was Nizām al-Dīn.

ghazal Lyric poem, generally of five or more *bayts* and in the rhyme scheme AA/BA/CA/DA. Includes the poet's *takhalluṣ* in the final *bayt*. Often erotic and mystical in subject, and closely related to Sufism. Derived historically from the *tashbib* section of a *qaṣīda*.

Ka'ba Sacred shrine; on the site of a shrine for pagan Arab gods.

Khāqānī (1121–99) Major poet of Persianate Azerbaijan; most famous for his prison poetry and *qaṣīdas* on Muslim-Christian themes.

Majnūn Male protagonist in an Arabian love story made famous by Niẓāmī of Ganja. Majnūn's name is also synonymous with love-madness in classical and contemporary Islamic languages and literatures.

malfūẓāt Compilation of sayings by a Sufi *shaykh*. Hasan authored the first South Asian *malfūẓāt*, *Fawā'id al-fu'ād* (*Benefits of the Heart*), concerning his teacher Nizām al-Dīn.

masnavī Persian verse narrative, or "romance"; in the rhyme scheme AA/BB/CC/DD.

maqṭa' (point of termination) Concluding verse of a *ghazal* that contains the poet's signature (*takhalluṣ*).

maṭla' (place of sunrise) Opening verse of a *ghazal* that rhymes in *misra's*; also means "refrain."

miṣrā' ("panel" in a home) Hemistich; two *misra'* constitute one *bayt* (couplet).

Nizām al-Dīn Awliya (1238–1325) The major Chishti *shaykh* of medieval India; teacher of both Hasan and Amīr Khusrow.

Niẓāmī (1141–1209)   Major Persian poet from Azerbaijan who pioneered the *masnavī* form and composed a *hamsa* (quintet) that included five *masnavīs*; imitated by many subsequent poets.

qaṣīda   Panegyric ode. The normative form for poetry in Arabic and Persian, from which the *ghazal* emerges.

qiṭaʿ (fragment)   Fragment; a short poem that does not fall into other genre rubrics. Typically grouped in its own section within a *dīwān*.

ravī   Rhyming letter in a *ghazal* or other Persian poem. Also called the *ḥarf-i qāfīye*.

rubāʿī   Quatrain in the AABA or AAAA rhyme scheme.

Saʿdī (d. 1291)   Major Persian poet from Shiraz; author of *Gulistān* (*Rose Garden*, in prose) and *Bustān* (also meaning *Rose Garden*, in verse). Amīr Khusrow called Hasan the "Saʿdī of Hindustan."

takhalluṣ   Pen name adopted by a poet in his verse. The *takhalluṣ* is generally repeated in the second to last line of Persian *ghazals*. The term also has the meaning of "exit verse."

Editions of Hasan's Work

Dīvān-i Ḥasan Sijzī Dihlavī: sadah-i haftum va hashtum. Ed. Aḥmad Bihishtī Shīrāzī and Ḥamīd Riẓā Qilīch Khānī. Tehran: Anjuman-i Āthār va Mafākhir-i Farhangī, 2004.

Divan. Ed. L. Z. Salomatshoeva. Dushanbe: Irfon, 1990. Persian texts with a helpful Russian introduction. Note that this scholar's name is spelled in more recent publications as Salomatshaeva.

Dīvān-i Amīr Ḥasan Sijzī Dihlavī. Ed. Nargīs Jahān. Delhi: Intisharat-i Ḥazrat Muhani Fā'undīshan, 2004.

Kitāb-i ʿishq. Ed. and trans. Aslam Farrukhī and Es. Em. Laṭifullāh. Karachi: Faẓlī Buk, 2000. An Urdu translation, alongside the Persian original and Urdu commentary.

Fawā'id al-fu'ād. Ed. Tawfīq Subḥānī. Tehran: Zuvvār, 1385/2006.

Hasan's Life and Work

Borah, M. I. "The Life and Works of Amir Hasan Dihlavi." *Journal of the Royal Asiatic Society of Bengal* 7 (1941): 1–59. Reprinted as *The Life and Works of Amir Hasan Dihlavi: A Thesis on the Famous Persian Literateur Amir Hasan Dihlavi, 1253–1328 A.D., based on original Persian sources & approved for the Ph.D. Degree in the University of London.* Guwahati, Assam: Govt. of India in the Dept. of Historical and Antiquarian Studies, 2001.

———. "A Short Account of an Unpublished Romantic *Masnavī* of Amir Ḥasan Dihlavī." *New Indian Antiquary* 2 (1939): 258–62.

Gould, Rebecca. "Persian Love in an Indian Environment: Ḥasan Sijzī's Metaphysics of Sexual Desire." In *Beloved: Love and Languishing in Middle Eastern Literatures and Cultures: A Volume of Essays.* Ed. Michael Beard, Alireza Korangy, and Hanadi al-Samman. London: I. B. Tauris, 2015.

Jahān, Nargīs. *Saʿdī-i-Hind: Hasan Dihlavī.* Delhi, 1989.

Nizami, K. A., and Bruce Lawrence. *Nizam al-Din Awliya: Morals for the Heart: Conversations of Shaykh Nizam ad-din Awliya Recorded by Amir Hasan Sijzi.* New York: Paulist Press, 1992.

Salomatshaeva, L. S. *Filosofskaia lirika Khasana Dekhlevi* [*The Philosophical Lyrics of Hasan of Delhi*]. Dushanbe: Donish, 1986. Note that the author's name is listed here as Salomatshaeva.

———. *Khasan Dekhlevi i simvolika ego gazelei.* Diss., Russian Academy of Sciences, Tajikistan, 2010.

Sharma, Sunil. "Hasan Sijzi and Amir Khusrau: Friends, Poets, and Devotees." In *Jashn-e-Khusrau 2013: Celebrating the Genius of Amir Khusrau.* Ed. Shakeel Hossain. Delhi: Aga Khan Trust for Culture, 2014. 77–87.

Pre-Mughal Indo-Persian Literature and Historiography

'Abdulghani, Muhammad. *Pre-Mughal Persian in Hindustan.* Allahabad: Allahabad Law Journal Press, 1941.

Aliev, G. Iu. *Persoiazychnaia literatura Indii. Kratkii ocherk.* Moscow: Nauka, 1968. Pages 65–69 are devoted to Hasan.

Baranī, Ziyā' al-Dīn. *Tārīkh-i firūzshāhī.* Ed. Sayyed Ahmad Khan. Calcutta, 1862.

Bednar, Michael. "The Content and the Form in Amīr Khusraw's Duval Rānī va Khizr Khān." *Journal of the Royal Asiatic Society* 21, no. 1 (2014): 17–35.

Dihlavī, Amīr Khusrow. *Duvalrānī Khazir Khān.* Ed. Mawlānā Rashīd Aḥmad Sālim Anṣarī and Khaliq Ahmad Nizami. Delhi: Idārah-'i Adabīyāt-i Dillī, 1988.

———. *Masnavī-i Tughluq'nāmah-yi Khusraw Dihlavī.* Ed. Sayyid Hāshimī Farīdābādī and Muhammad Ṣadīq Hasan. Awrangābād: Maṭba'-i Urdū, 1933.

———. *Nuh sipihr.* Ed. Mohammad Wahid Mirza. London: Oxford University Press, 1950.

Gabbay, Alyssa. *Islamic Tolerance: Amir Khusraw and Pluralism.* London: Routledge, 2010.

Habib, Mohammad, and Umar Salim Khan Afshar. *The Political Theory of the Delhi Sultanate.* Allahabad, 1961. A partial translation of Ziā'-al-Din Barani's *Fatāwā-ye jahāndāri.*

Hardy, Peter. *Historians of Medieval India: Studies in Indo-Muslim Historical Writing.* London: Luzac, 1960.

'Iṣāmi, 'Abd-al-Malek. *Fotuh al-salāṭin.* Ed. A. S. Usha. Madras, 1948. Trans. Agha Mahdi Husain. *Futūḥu's-Salāṭīn or Shah Namah-i Hind.* Aligarh, 1967–77.

Kirmani, Waris, ed. *Dreams Forgotten: An Anthology of Indo-Persian Poetry.* Aligarh: Kitab-khana-yi Shiraz, 1986.

Kirmani, Waris. "Amir Khusrau—The Founder of Indo-Persian Ghazal." *Indo-Iranica* 41, nos. 1–4 (1988): 97–108.

Lawrence, Bruce. *Notes from a Distant Flute: The Extant Literature of Pre-Mughal Indian Sufism.* Tehran: Imperial Iranian University of Philosophy, 1978.

Losensky, Paul, and Sunil Sharma. *In the Bazaar of Love: The Selected Poetry of Amir Khusrau.* Delhi: Penguin Books India, 2011. With introduction, pp. xi–liii.

Mohammad, Wahid Mirza. *The Life and Works of Amir Khusrau: Thesis Submitted for the PhD Degree of the London University in 1929.* 1935; reprint, Lahore, 1962.

Nuʿmani Shibli. *Shiʿr al-ʿAjam.* Trans. [from Urdu into Persian] Taqī Fakhr Dāʿī Gīlānī. Tehran: Ibn Sina, 1335/1956/7.

Sharma, Sunil. *Amir Khusraw: The Poet of Sultans and Sufis.* Oxford: One World Books, 2005.

———. "Amir Khusraw and the Genre of Historical Narratives in Verse." *Comparative Studies of South Asia, Africa and the Middle East* 22, no. 1 (2003): 112–18.

———. "Literary Aspects of Amir Khusrau's Poetry." In *Jashn-e Khusraw: A Collection.* Ed. Shakeel Hossain. New Delhi: Aga Khan Trust for Culture, 2012, 70–95.

Thapar, Romila. *Somanatha: The Many Voices of a History.* Delhi: Penguin Books India, 2004.

Chishti Sufism

Alam Muzaffar. "The Debate Within: A Sufi Critique of Religious Law, Tasawwuf and Politics in Mughal India." *South Asian History and Culture* 2, no. 2 (2011): 138–59.

Ernst, Carl W., and Bruce B. Lawrence, eds. *Sufi Martyrs of Love: The Chishti Order in South Asia and Beyond.* New York: Palgrave, 2002. Strongest on the contemporary period.

Lawrence, Bruce B. "Honoring Women through Sexual Abstinence: Lessons from the Spiritual Practice of a Pre-modern South Asian Sufi Master, Shaykh Nizam ad-din Awliya." In *Festschrift for Annemarie Schimmel.* Ed. Maria Subtelny. *Journal of Turkish Studies* 18 (1994): 149–61.

Nizami, Khaliq Ahmad. "Early Indo-Muslim Mystics and Their Attitude towards the State." *Islamic Culture* 22 (1948): 387–98; 23 (1949): 12–32, 162–70, 312–24; 24 (1950): 60–71.

Taneeva-Salomatshaeva, L. Z. *Istoki sufizma v srednevekovoi Indii: bratstvo Chishtiia* [*Sources of Sufism in Medieval India: The Chishti Brotherhood*]. Moscow: Vostochnaia literatura RAN, 2009. The author is the same as L. Z. Salomatshaeva, the leading Tajik expert on Hasan's *ghazals*.

The Delhi Sultanate

Auer, Blain. *Symbols of Authority in Medieval Islam: History, Religion and Muslim Legitimacy in the Delhi Sultanate*. London: I. B. Tauris, 2012.

Digby, Simon. "The Sufi Shaykh and the Sultan: A Conflict of Claims to Authority in Medieval India." *Iran* 28 (1990): 71–81.

———. "The Sufi Shaykh as a Source of Authority in Medieval India." *Purusartha, Islam et société en asie du sud* (1986): 57–77.

Jackson, Peter. *The Delhi Sultanate: A Political and Military History*. Cambridge: Cambridge University Press, 1999.

Kumar, Sunil. "Assertions of Authority: A Study of the Discursive Statements of Two Sultans of Delhi." In *The Making of Indo-Persian Culture: Indian and French Studies*. Ed. Muzaffar Alam, Françoise "Nalini" Delvoye, and Marc Gabourieau. Delhi: Centre de Sciences Humaines, 2000, 37–65.

———. *The Emergence of the Delhi Sultanate, 1192–1286*. Delhi: Permanent Black, 2010.

Nizami, Khaliq Ahmad. *On History and Historians of Medieval India*. Delhi: Munshiram Manoharlal, 1983.

Prasad, Pushpa. *Sanskrit Inscriptions of Delhi Sultanate, 1191–1526*. Delhi: Oxford University Press, 1990.

Sarkar, Nilanjan. "An Urban *Imaginaire*, ca. 1350: The Capital City in Ziya' Barani's *Fatawa-i Jahandari*." *Indian Economic & Social History Review* 48 (2011): 407–24.

The Ghazal and Other Lyric Genres

Bauer, Thomas, and Angelika Neuwirth, eds. *Ghazal as World Literature*. Beirut: Orient-Institut, 2005.

Davis, Dick. *Borrowed Ware: Medieval Persian Epigrams*. London: Anvil Press Poetry, 2004.

———. *Faces of Love: Hafez and the Poets of Shiraz*. Washington, D.C.: Mage Publishers, 2012.

Fatima, Rais. *Ghazal under the Umayyads*. New Delhi: Kitab Bhavan, 1995.

Ingenito, Domenico. "Tabrizis in Shiraz Are Worth Less than a Dog: Sa'dī and Humām, a Lyrical Encounter." In *Politics, Patronage and the Trans-*

mission of Knowledge in 13th-15th Century Tabriz. Ed. Judith Pfeiffer. Leiden: Brill, 2014. 77-128.

Jacobi, Renate. "Theme and Variations in Umayyad Ghazal Poetry." *Journal of Arabic Literature* 23, no. 2 (1992): 109-19.

————. "Time and Reality in Nasib and Ghazal." *Journal of Arabic Literature* 16 (1985): 1-17.

Kinany, A. Kh. *The Development of Gazal in Arabic Literature: Pre-Islamic and Early Islamic Periods.* Damascus: Syrian University Printing House, 1950.

Korangy, Alireza. *Development of the Ghazal and Khaqani's Contribution: A Study of the Development of Ghazal and a Literary Exegesis of a 12th c. Poetic Harbinger.* Wiesbaden: Harrassowitz Verlag, 2013.

Shackle, Christopher. "Ghazal." *Keywords in South Asian Studies.* Online project initiated by Rachel Dwyer, School of African and Oriental Studies. http://www.soas.ac.uk/ssai/keywords

For their manifold generosity, kindness, and various forms of inspiration, I extend my heartfelt thanks to my friends and colleagues: Muzaffar Alam, Barney Bate, Allison Busch, Alexander Key, Alireza Korangy, Frank Lewis, Arvind Mehotra, Matthew Miller, Francesca Orsini, Sheldon Pollock, Pranav Prakash, Harsha Ram, and Sunil Sharma. I wish to express particular thanks to Éva Gönczi and Éva Fodor of Central European University's Institute for Advanced Studies, where much of this manuscript was completed with the help of a Senior Research Fellowship. I will always remember with fondness the wonderful intellectual atmosphere they succeeded in creating for fellows during 2014–15 academic year. In my early days at the University of Bristol, Robert Villain, Carol O'Sullivan, and Susan Harrow created a wonderful environment for pursuing scholarship and teaching in translation studies.

I am most grateful to Mike Levine, my editor at Northwestern University Press, who suggested this project to me, and without whom it would never have come into existence. I also wish to express my gratitude to the entire staff at Northwestern University Press, especially to Anne Gendler, and to copyeditor Lys Ann Weiss, who helped to perfect the text.

Any translation of this scale is necessarily a work in progress, and I ask the reader's indulgence for all infelicities, which will be corrected in future editions.